Stock Trading Secrets

A beginners guide to profit
From the Stock Market

Dylan Schlotmann

Copyright 2022. All Rights Reserved.

This document provides exact and reliable information regarding the topic and issues covered. The publication is sold with the idea that the publisher is not required to render accounting, officially permitted, or otherwise qualified services. If advice is necessary, legal or professional, a practiced individual in the profession should be ordered.

From a Declaration of Principles which was accepted and approved equally by a Committee of the American Bar Association and a Committee of Publishers and Associations.

In no way is it legal to reproduce, duplicate, or transmit any part of this document in either electronic means or printed format. Recording of this publication is strictly prohibited, and any storage of this document is not allowed unless with written permission from the publisher. All rights reserved.

The information provided herein is stated to be truthful and consistent. Any liability, in terms of inattention or otherwise, by any usage or abuse of any policies, processes, or Instructions contained within is the solitary and utter responsibility of the recipient reader.

Under no circumstances will any legal obligation or blame be held against the publisher for reparation, damages, or monetary loss due to the information herein, either directly or indirectly.

Respective authors own all copyrights not held by the publisher.

The information herein is offered for informational purposes solely and is universal as such. The presentation of the data is without a contract or any guarantee assurance.

TABLE OF contentS

Introduction

Stock trading explained

Common stock trading terminology

Stock order types (what you must know)

Stock trading secrets that nobody tells you

Three types of trends every trader should know

Area of value: How to buy low and sell high

Entry triggers: Price patterns to better time your entry

Exits: How to protect your downside and maximize your profits

Risk management and position sizing

The truth about risk-to-reward ratio

Stock trading strategies that work

Trade sweeteners

How to develop a trading plan to improve your trading results

How to choose a good stockbroker

Seven common stock trading mistakes to avoid

Final words

Acknowledgments

INTRODUCTION

When I was 19 years old, I served in the army as a commando. Back then, one of our graduation requirements was to complete a 72 km (45 mi) road march—in 24 hours.

This meant we wouldn't be sleeping during the night, and we would be walking till we clocked the full 72 km. And of course, we'd be doing it in full battle order (meaning we'd be carrying our field packs and weapons).

So, we started at noon, just after having lunch. The first 4 km (2.5 mi) was easy. The next 4 km was easy. Another 4 km, easy.

At the 13 km (8 mi) mark, BAM!—I pulled a tendon behind my knee cap. "Shit," I thought to myself.

On a scale of 1 to 10, the pain was around a 4. I had no idea how long it would last or if it would get worse. I remember saying to myself:

"One step at a time, baby."

"Let's see where this goes."

"I'm either going to be a hero, or I'm heading back to my bunk with a zero."

So, I marched on. Interestingly, I became accustomed to the pain to the point where it seemed like "second nature" to me. So I continued…

At the 35 km (22 mi) mark, we had a 60-minute break. Boy, I didn't know sitting down could feel SO GOOD. I rested my aching feet, had a cheeseburger (courtesy of my parents), and shut my eyes. The next thing I knew, our break was up, and we had to get moving again (I swear those were the fastest 60 minutes of my life).

So, I packed my stuff. Stood up. And took my first step… *OUCH.*

It felt like I was walking on broken glass. That's because I had blisters on the soles of my feet. As I walked, I pressed against those blisters, and it felt as if they were about to explode.

On a pain level, I'd say it was an 8 out of 10. I told myself: "One step at a time."

"If everyone else can do it, so can I."

"I'm not chickening out here. At least not yet."

So I bit my lip and pressed on. The next 10 km (6 mi) was sheer torture as I dragged my blistered feet forward, step-by-step. Slowly, my body adapted to the pain. Yes, my feet still hurt like hell. But I had come to embrace the pain. So, I marched on and reached the 70 km (44 mi) mark.

STOCK TRADING
explained

When I was seven years old, I was always at my aunt's house because there was no one to take care of me during the day.

As I recall, she was always watching television. However, she wasn't watching sitcoms, dramas, or the news. Instead, she was staring at a bunch of numbers on the screen that blinked every 15 minutes.

Now, because the numbers only blinked every 15 minutes, she would often fall asleep in front of the television, only to be jolted awake (as if by sudden thunder) to check if the numbers on the screen had changed. If they hadn't, she went back to napping.

Now you're probably wondering, "What did the numbers mean?" It wasn't until many years later that I realized she was watching something called Teletext—which displays stock prices on your television.

And unlike the Teletext that put my aunt to sleep, I'll do my best to ensure the same thing doesn't happen to you while you're reading this book. I'll keep things concise, provide a summary of each chapter, and share some interesting stories with you along the way. Cool? Then let's get started…

WHAT IS A STOCK?

A stock represents ownership of a company. You're probably thinking, "What, I own the company?!" Yes, you do. But only an extremely small part of it. Let me give you an example…

As of October 2021, Apple had

- Market capitalization: $2,494.5 billion
- 16.63 billion shares outstanding
- Stock price: $150

So, if you were to buy 1 of 11 share of Apple stock now, it would cost you $150. And you'd own 1 / 16.63 billionth of Apple. Clearly, your % ownership of Apple would be extremely small, but still, you'd be an owner. Here's why…

If Apple earned a profit, you'd get a cut of it, either through dividends or capital gains (when the stock price goes up). Likewise, if Apple were losing money, the stock price would go down, and you'd suffer a loss. Does this make sense? Great. Now that you understand what a stock is, let's learn more about the different types of stocks out there…

TYPES OF STOCKS

There are two primary ways you can classify stocks, either through market capitalization or stock sectors. Let me explain...

Market capitalization

Market capitalization measures how much a company is worth. It's calculated by multiplying the total number of shares by the current stock price. For example, at the time of writing, Apple is worth a staggering $2,494.5 billion (calculation: 16.63 billion x $150 = $2,494.5 billion).

And since Apple's market capitalization is greater than $200 billion, it's considered a mega cap. Now, not all companies are as big as Apple, and that's why we have different categories of market capitalization. Here's the full breakdown...

- Mega Cap > $200 billion
- Large Cap > $10 billion
- Mid Cap = $2 billion to $10 billion
- Small Cap = $300 million to $2

billion
- Micro Cap = $50 million to $300 million
- Nano Cap < $50 million

Beyond market capitalization, you can also classify stocks according to their sector...

Stock sector

A stock sector is a group of stocks attached to companies in a similar industry. For example, Microsoft and Google belong to the information technology sector, JPMorgan and Goldman Sachs belong to the financial sector, and so on.

According to the Global Industry Classification Standard (GICS), you can classify stocks into 1 of 11 sectors:

1. Energy
2. Materials
3. Industrials

4. Utilities
5. Healthcare
6. Financials
7. Consumer Discretionary
8. Consumer Staples
9. Information Technology
10. Communication Services
11. Real Estate

Moving on, let's find out who the participants in the stock market are...

THE PARTICIPANTS IN THE STOCK MARKET

Retail traders: This refers to individuals who trade with their own money.

Hedge funds: Hedge funds can be run either by corporations or companies that manage other people's money. They can trade across multiple asset classes (like the stock market) and employ complex trading strategies.

Institutions: There are many types of institutions that invest in the stock market. One example is insurance companies, which use the premiums they collect to invest in the stock market.

Stockbrokers: In the 1980s, it was common for stockbrokers to help retail traders facilitate their trades. For example, if you wanted to buy 100 shares of Microsoft, you'd call your broker and he'd execute the trade for you—and earn a commission. But as technology improved, there was little need for brokers anymore.

Market makers: Before the rise of electronic trading, market makers were people who provided liquidity in the market. This means when you bought/sold, there'd be someone on the other side to take your trade. But as technology improved, market makers were replaced by machines that could do a much better job.

High-frequency traders (HFTs): This is done by machines that can execute thousands of trades each day. Their purpose is to provide liquidity in the market and to earn a profit while doing so.

So you've learned who the participants in the stock market are. But what makes this market so attractive? Let's find out...

ADVANTAGES OF THE STOCK MARKET

There are four key advantages when it comes to the stock market...

Bias towards the upside

Most stock markets around the world have an upward bias. That's because, as the economy progresses, people earn more income. And with a greater income, they can spend more, which means higher earnings for companies. And when a company has higher earnings, this leads to a higher stock price. That's why, in the long run, most stock markets are in an uptrend.

So, how is this an advantage for you? Well, it makes your trading easier because you don't have to worry about shorting the markets. Instead, focus on buying stocks in an uptrend because they're likely to continue moving higher. I'll show you how to do this later, but for now, let's move on…

More trading opportunities

Unlike the Forex market, where you have a limited number of currency pairs, the stock market has thousands of stocks to choose from. This offers you more trading opportunities and greater profit potential. If a stock doesn't meet your criteria, then move on. You've got thousands of stocks to choose from—which means you never have to force a trade.

Easier to understand

Among the various financial instruments out there, the stock market is probably the easiest to understand because it's made up of companies you're already familiar with. And if you understand how a company makes money, you're likely to buy the stock.

For example, if you watch Netflix, then you know the company makes money through subscriptions. So if you think that's a great business to be in, you can buy the stock and own a piece of Netflix (albeit a small one).

Lower risk

Unlike the Forex market, where you need leverage because most currency pairs don't move a lot day to day, the stock market doesn't require leverage. That's because stocks are more volatile, and you can get a decent return without leverage.

And without leverage, the chances of blowing up your account are lower because the stock needs to go to zero for this to happen (and if you trade multiple stocks, all of them need to go to zero before you're completely wiped out).

Something for everyone

The stock market suits traders with a range of different risk appetites. Let's say you want to trade stocks with higher volatility; you can focus on micro cap or small-cap stocks. And if you want a stock that's less volatile and more stable, you can focus on large cap or mega cap stocks.

Or perhaps you think technology companies are the future. Then you can focus on stocks in the information technology sector. So no matter what "theme" you're looking for, you can probably find it in the stock market.

Next, you'll discover what a stock exchange is and how it works…

WHAT IS A STOCK EXCHANGE?

A stock exchange is like a marketplace. It has both buyers and sellers, and it benefits both parties because sellers can easily sell their goods and buyers can easily find something that suits them.

In other words, a stock exchange helps facilitate transactions between buyers and sellers. And that's not all. A stock exchange also has these benefits…

It saves you a lot of hassle

If there were no stock exchange, then you'd have to go directly to a company to buy their stock. Imagine that you wanted to buy stock from 20 different companies, and they were located all around the world—buying stock from all these companies would be a nightmare!

It lowers your risk of fraud

To be listed on a stock exchange, a company has to submit their financial reports and follow other regulatory requirements—which allows investors to better understand the business. Companies that fail to do this won't be listed on the exchange. In other words, the stock exchange helps you filter companies that run their businesses properly from those that are outright scams.

There are no counterparty risks

Imagine you had 100 shares of Google, and you wanted to sell them. Then a stranger came along and said, "Hey I'm looking to buy Google! Why don't I buy 100 shares from you?" There would be a few problems with this. For example, how could you be sure the stranger would pay? What if he took your shares and disappeared into thin air? What if the price of Google suddenly increased? Would you sell him the shares at the "new" price or the "old" price? You can clearly see where I'm coming from.

But the good news is, this doesn't happen when you trade on the stock exchange because there are mechanisms in place that solve these issues. Whew!

There are many stock exchanges around the world. But at the time of writing, the three biggest ones are…

1. New York Stock Exchange (NYSE)
2. Nasdaq
3. Shanghai Stock Exchange (SSE)

At this point, you've learned what a stock is. You've also learned about the different types of stocks and participants that make up the stock market, and what the advantages of having an exchange are. In the next chapter, you'll learn some common stock trading terminology so you don't get lost in a sea of technical jargon.

SUMMARY

- A stock represents ownership in a company. If you own one share of Apple, technically, you own part of the company, albeit a really small one.

- You can classify stocks according to their market capitalization or the sector they're in.

- Participants in the stock market include retail traders, hedge funds, institutions, stockbrokers, market makers, high-frequency traders, etc.

- Advantages of the stock market include long-run upside bias, plenty of trading opportunities, ease of understanding, and lower risk. In addition, the stock market appeals to traders with different goals or risk appetites.

- A stock exchange is like a

marketplace. It connects both buyers and sellers, thus making it easy for them to "do business" with one another.

COMMON STOCK TRADING
terminology

One day while I was working out at the gym, I heard a bunch of students speaking English, but I couldn't make sense of what they were saying. They were using words like "sus," "swol," and "salty." Later, I realized these were the terms (or lingo) used by their generation. If you ask me, these words will likely be irrelevant in a few years.

And in case you're wondering...

sus = suspicious

swol = muscular

salty = jealous

Anyway, the terminology we use in the stock market will likely remain the same. So let's get right to it...

What is a stock symbol?

Let's say you want to trade McDonald's stock. It's a hassle to type the full name "McDonald's." So to make your life easier, you can type the stock symbol instead—"MCD." And that's what a stock symbol is; it's a series of letters used to represent the name of the stock. Also, every stock symbol is unique and its length can vary from one to five letters. Here are some examples...

- Google (GOOG)
- Netflix (NFLX)
- Alcoa Corp (AA)
- Morgan Stanley (MS)
- Cloudflare (NET)

Next, let's learn what a tick is...

WHAT IS A TICK?

A tick is the minimum price movement of a stock. For stocks trading above $1,

1 tick is $0.01. For example, if the stock price of Apple moves from $100 to $100.05, this means it has increased by 5 ticks (or 5 cents). Moving on...

WHAT ARE LONG AND SHORT?

When you're long a stock, it means you bought a stock, and you're bullish on it. You'll make a profit if the price moves higher. On the other hand...

When you're short a stock, it means you sold the stock, and you're bearish on it. You'll make a profit if the price goes lower. Now you might be wondering, "How does short-selling work?" Let me explain...

When you short a stock, it means you've sold the stock. But how do you sell stock that you don't own? Well, you borrow it from your broker, and you have to return it later.

For example, let's say you shorted 100 shares of Netflix at $200. When you sell something, you'll get the proceeds back. In this case, $20,000 in cash will be transferred to your account (calculation: 100 x $200 = $20,000). But remember, you have to return the stock to your broker because you borrowed it.

Now, let's say the price of Netflix drops to $190, and you want to cover (or exit) your short trade. To do this, you have to buy back the Netflix stock so you can return it to your broker. So you buy 100 shares of Netflix at $190. This costs you $19,000 (calculation: 100 x $190 = $19,000).

Your net profit on this trade is $1000 (calculation $20,000 - $19,000 = $1,000).

Of course, if the stock price of Netflix goes up, you'll lose money. And technically, your losses are infinite because there's no cap on how high the price of Netflix can go.

Now if you're new to trading, I recommend staying away from short-selling because you risk unlimited losses. Plus, the stock market has an inherent upside bias, which means it's easier to make money on the long side than the short. I'll talk more about this later, but for now, let's move on and learn about the bid, the ask, and the spread…

WHAT ARE THE BID, THE ASK, AND THE SPREAD, AND WHY DO THEY MATTER?

When you trade any financial market (whether it's stocks, Forex, futures, etc.), you'll encounter two prices on your charts—the bid and the ask. Let me explain…

Bid price

The bid is the price you can sell your stock for on the market right now. So if you want to exit a long position or short a stock, you'll refer to the bid price.

Here's an example of the bid price on TradingView charting platform…

Figure 3.1 – The bid price

As you can see, the bid price of Tesla is 1127.30. So if you want to exit a long position (or if you want to short Tesla), you can do so at the current bid price.

Ask price

The ask is the price you can buy stock for on the market right now. So if you want to exit a short position or long a stock, you'll refer to the ask price. Here's an example of the ask price on TradingView charting platform…

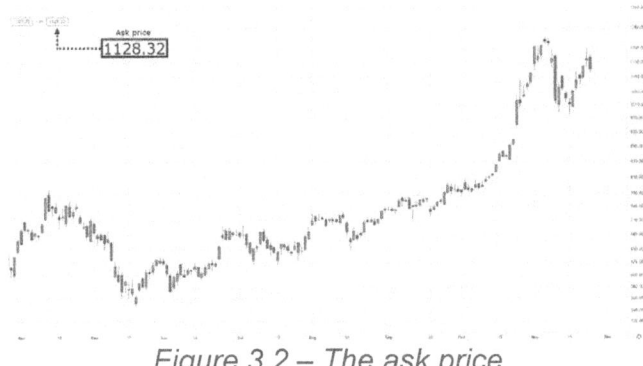

Figure 3.2 – The ask price

As you can see, the ask price of Tesla is 1128.32. So if you want to exit a short position (or if you want to go long on Tesla), you can do so at the current ask price.

The spread

The spread is the difference between the ask and the bid price. For example, if the ask price on Tesla is $1000.55 and the bid price is $1000.50, then the spread is 5 cents (calculation $1000.55 - $1000.50 = $0.05).

Now, you might be thinking, "Why does the spread matter?" The spread matters because it's your transaction cost. If the spread is wider, it means your transaction cost is higher. Here's how it works...

Example 1

- You bought 100 shares of Apple with a spread of $1.
- How much did the spread cost you?

Well, it cost you $100 (calculation: 100 × $1 = $100). In other words, you were down $100 the moment you bought 100 shares of Apple. Here's another one...

Example 2

- You bought 100 shares of Apple with a spread of $0.01.
- How much did the spread cost you?

Well, it cost you $1 (calculation: 100 × $0.01 = $1). Can you see how the spread has an impact on your trading?

The wider the spread, the higher your transaction cost. So how can you lower your transaction costs in stock trading?

HOW TO REDUCE YOUR TRANSACTION COSTS

There are two ways to lower your transaction costs:

1. Trading stocks with higher liquidity
2. Trading the higher timeframe

1: Trading stocks with higher liquidity

Liquidity refers to how easy it is to buy or sell a stock at your desired price. Stocks with larger market capitalization have a tighter spread because there's more interest from market participants (and that improves liquidity).

As of this writing, the spread on Apple is 0.01, as shown below…

Figure 3.3 – A spread of $0.01 on Apple

Now, compare this to a stock like Uranium Energy Corp, where the spread is 1.21, as shown below…

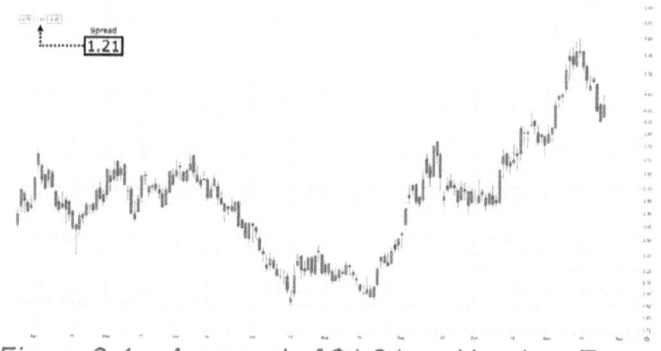

Figure 3.4 – A spread of $1.21 on Uranium Energy Corp

In other words, if you want to reduce your transaction costs, focus on trading stocks with a larger market capitalization (like $10 billion and above). Moving on…

2: Trading the higher timeframe

When you trade on the higher timeframe, you'll use a wider stop loss to accommodate the wider swings of the market. And with a wider stop loss, the relative cost of the spread is lower (in contrast, when you trade on the lower timeframe, the cost is higher).

This is best explained with an example, so let's get to it…

Example 1: Trading on the lower timeframe

- Stop loss: $1
- Spread: $0.1
- Risk on the trade: $500
- Position size: 500 shares

In this case, the spread "eats up" 10% (calculation $0.1 / $1 = 10%) of your stop loss. This means when you put on a trade, you're instantly down 10% of what you're risking. In this example, you've risked $500 on the trade and paid $50 to the spread.

Example 2: Trading on the higher timeframe

- Stop loss: $10
- Spread: $0.1
- Risk on the trade: $500
- Position size: 50 shares

In this case, the spread is 1% of your stop loss (calculation $0.1 / $10 = 1%). This means when you put on a trade, you're only down 1% of what you're risking. In this example, you risked $500 on the trade and paid $5 to the spread.

(Note: The reason you traded 50 shares in this scenario is because you had a wider stop loss. So if you want to risk the same $500 on the trade, then you have to reduce your position size accordingly. We'll cover risk management and position sizing in more detail later.)

At this point, you've learned some common stock trading terminology. In the next chapter, you'll discover what the different stock order types are and when to use them.

SUMMARY

- A stock symbol is a series of letters used to represent the name of the stock.

- A tick is the minimum price movement of a stock. For stock above $1, one tick equals $0.01.

- Long means you're bullish, and you'll make a profit if the stock price moves higher.

- Short means you're bearish, and you'll make a profit if the stock price moves lower.

- The bid is the price you can sell at right now, and the ask is the price you can buy at right now.

- The spread is the difference between the ask and bid. The wider the spread, the higher your transaction cost.

- To reduce your transaction cost,

you can trade stocks with larger capitalization or trade on the higher timeframe.

STOCK ORDER TYPES (what you must know)

In 2012, I was a proprietary trader (someone who trades the firm's money and is compensated based on the amount of profit they generate), and I was instructed to use an expensive trading software that cost $1000/month.

I recall feeling dumbfounded when I wanted to place an order in the market. Why? Because there were so many ways to do it. You've got things like machine gun order, iceberg order, time-sliced order, conditional order, sniper order, and so on. So I spent a ton of time learning these different order types.

The good news is, you don't have to go through all that because, as a retail trader, you only need to know these four order types...

1. Market order
2. Limit order
3. Stop order
4. Stop-loss order

So let me explain what they are, how they work, and the pros and cons of each...

1: MARKET ORDER

A market order is used when you want to enter a trade immediately, no matter what.

For example, Amazon is trading at $100, and you want to buy 100 shares of it using a market order. This means you're telling your broker that you want to buy 100 shares of Amazon at the current price no matter what (even if the price goes higher).

Advantage: You're guaranteed to be in the trade no matter what.

Disadvantage: In fast-moving markets, you could end up paying a higher-than-expected price.

So, when do you use a market order? They're commonly used when you have a valid trading setup and want to enter a trade as soon as possible, before the market "runs away."

2: LIMIT ORDER

A limit order is used when you want to enter at a "better" price than the one that's currently quoted.

For example, Google is trading at $200. You think the price is too high, and you'll only buy it at $150. So you place a buy limit order at $150. This means if the price of Google drops to $150, you'll buy Google at $150. If not, there's no trade.

Advantage: You get to specify the price you want to enter at.

Disadvantage: There's no guarantee your limit order will be filled.

So when do you use a limit order? They're commonly used when you want to get in at a specific price or better. Here's a real-world example…

Figure 4.1 – A buy limit order

Cheniere Energy (LNG) is in an uptrend on the daily timeframe. However, the price is approaching the highs, and you don't want to buy when the price is this high. Instead, you want to buy near support (a concept I'll explain shortly) because you expect buying pressure to step in. The nearest support is at $102, so you place a buy limit order at $102.

3: STOP ORDER

A stop order is used when you want to get into a trade only if the market has reached a specific price level.

For example, Netflix is trading between $110 and $120. You want to buy at the breakout if the price goes above $120. So you place a buy stop order five ticks above the high, at $120.05. This means if the price of Netflix reaches $120.05, you'll automatically buy Netflix. If not, there's no trade.

You're probably wondering, "What's the difference between a buy limit order and a buy stop order?" A buy limit order is used when you want to enter at a price *below* the current market price (e.g., buying on a pullback). A buy stop order is used when you want to enter at a price *above* the current market price (e.g., buying on a breakout). Make sense?

Advantage: You're entering with upward momentum at your back.

Disadvantage: It could be a false breakout.

So when do you use a stop order? Stop orders are commonly used when you want to trade breakouts. Here's a real-world example...

Figure 4.2 – A buy stop order

Zurn Water Solutions (ZWS) is in an uptrend on the daily timeframe. As you can see, the price is within the highs and lows between $35.05 and $38.30. You believe that if the price can break out of the consolidation, there's a good chance of it moving higher. So, you place a buy stop order five ticks above the high—at $38.35.

There's no rule that says you must set your buy stop order five ticks above the high. It's up to you. If you want, you can even set it one tick above the high.

4: STOP-LOSS ORDER

Unlike the earlier order types that get you into a trade, a stop-loss order is an order that gets you out of a trade. Stop-loss orders are used if you want to exit a losing trade when the market has reached a specific price level.

For example, you bought Coca-Cola at $50, and your stop loss is at $48. Now, if the market moves against you and trades to a low of $48, your stop-loss order will automatically exit your trade at a loss of $2.

Advantage: You cut your losses so you can live to fight another day.

Disadvantage: You might get stopped out prematurely, only to watch the market move back in your intended direction.

So when do you use a stop-loss order? On every trade, because you have no idea whether the next trade will be a winner or a loser. Here's a real-world example…

Figure 4.3 – A stop-loss order

You bought Alcoa near support at $46. At the same time, you know there's a possibility the price could break lower. So, you place your stop loss at $43.

This means if the stock price drops to a low of $43, you'll immediately exit the trade.

WHAT IS SLIPPAGE?

Slippage occurs when the expected price and the executed price are different. For example, let's say you saw Apple last traded at $100. You entered a market order to buy 100 shares of Apple, but your trade was executed at $100.05 instead of the $100 you expected. That's a negative slippage of $0.05 per share (calculation: $100.05 - $100 = $0.05).

Slippage can also be positive. For example, let's say you saw that Google was last traded at $50. You enter a market order to buy 200 shares of Google, and your trade is executed at $49.98 instead of the $50 you expected. That's a positive slippage of $0.02.

WHY DOES SLIPPAGE OCCUR?

Slippage usually occurs in low-liquid markets or when there's high-impact news coming up. In this type of market environment, there's a lack of orders (bid and ask) on the order book. If you want to place a buy order in this situation, there might not be enough sellers on the opposite end to take your trade. So what happens? The price moves higher to attract sellers to take the opposite side of your trade, and that's when slippage occurs.

HOW CAN YOU AVOID SLIPPAGE?

Now you can't avoid slippage entirely, but there are things you can do to minimize it.

1: Use limit orders

A limit order specifies the exact price (or better) you'll enter a trade at. If the price goes up, a limit order won't have you chasing the higher price, which means you get little or no slippage.

2: Trade larger market capitalization stocks

Stocks with a larger market capitalization are more liquid because there's more interest. This means more buyers and sellers will be trading with one another, which reduces slippage.

3: Avoid trading during high-impact news releases

Just before a high-impact news release, the order book is thin. That's because traders remove their orders to avoid getting caught in the wrong market direction. So if you want to avoid slippage, avoid trading during high-impact news releases.

At this point, you've learned what the different stock order types are and how they work. In the next chapter, you'll discover stock trading secrets that nobody tells you.

SUMMARY

- A market order gets you into a trade immediately, no matter what.

- A buy limit order gets you into a trade only if the price drops to a specific level. And a sell limit order gets you into a trade only if the price rises to a specific level.

- A buy stop order gets you into a trade only if the price moves up to a specific level. And a sell stop order gets you into a trade only if the price drops to a specific level.

- A stop-loss order gets you out of a trade when the market has reached a specific level against you.

- Slippage occurs when the expected price and the executed price are different.

- To avoid slippage, use limit orders, trade stocks with larger market capitalization, and avoid trading during high-impact news releases.

STOCK TRADING SECRETS
that nobody tells you

Many years ago, I served in the army as a commando.

And one of my requirements before graduation was to navigate through a swamp in Brunei. Here's how it started…

6 a.m.

We took a boat in the early hours of the morning and headed towards a swamp. In order to make it out the same day, we had to complete the swamp walk by 5 p.m. and take the boat back to camp.

If you didn't make it out on time, you'd have to stay in the swamp overnight and take the boat back to camp the next morning. As you might imagine, no one wanted to stay in the swamp overnight.

7 a.m.

We reached the entrance of the swamp. There was no "ladder" or any assistance whatsoever to help you off the boat. You had to simply jump off the boat into the swamp. I did just that, and something caught me by surprise…

My whole body sank into the swamp—and I found myself standing up to my waist in mud.

(FYI: I'm 1.8 m (5 ft, 9 in) tall, and the mud was level with my belly button. I can't imagine what it was like for people who were 1.7 m; the mud was probably up to their chest or higher. Gulp!)

As you can imagine, when you're stuck that deep in the mud, it's hard to move forward. Each step took a lot of strength because you had to "battle" against the sticky mud (it's like walking in water but three times harder because mud is thicker).

After an hour of walking through the mud, guess how much ground we had covered? One hundred meters (109.36 yds)—it was pathetic.

As the hours passed, I started to feel weird. I noticed this tingling sensation on my face. Then I saw one of my buddies looking at me with a shocked expression. "Bro, what's wrong with your face?" he asked.

I took out my pocket mirror and realized that my face was swollen. *WTF!* Then I checked my arms. They had patches of red all over them—I was covered in a rash.

I thought to myself, "Shit, this isn't good."

Now, every step forward seemed more difficult than the last. That's when it dawned on me that I was gasping for air. And I thought to myself, "Oh f***!"

I quickly sat down, resting my back against a tree so I could catch my breath. I tried drinking lots of water. And I rested for a good 10 minutes. But still, nothing seemed to work.

That's when my officer decided to call for help to get me back to camp. The problem was ... we were in the middle of a swamp!

Heli-Casevac wouldn't work because the helicopter couldn't fly in. Getting out by boat wasn't an option because a boat wouldn't be able to penetrate the swamp. I had two choices...

Either I pulled my shit together—or I died. I wondered to myself, "Oh god, is this the end?"

Fortunately, I had a smart medic on my team. He quickly issued me some hydration salts, an orange powder you dissolve in water to replenish your nutrient levels.

I drank a packet dissolved in water and instantly felt better. "Damn, this stuff works like magic!" I thought. So I quickly chugged two more packets. Slowly, the breathlessness lifted. *Whew!*

(As it turned out, my body was low on sugar.)

Once I was feeling better, I quickly started walking again so I wouldn't have to spend the night in the swamp. Eventually, I made it out of the swamp—alive. *Booyah!*

What I learned as a result of this experience was that when we're carried away by the tasks at hand, we sometimes neglect the fundamentals—and the same goes for trading.

That's why, right now, you're learning the fundamentals of profitable stock trading so you won't constantly be on a hamster wheel chasing the latest fads, indicators, strategies, and whatnot. So let's go...

1: THE US STOCK MARKET IS IN A LONG-TERM UPTREND

Don't take my word for it. Have a look at the S&P 500 over the last 10 years...

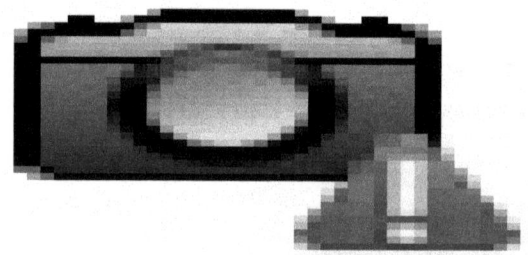

Figure 5.1 – S&P 500 in an uptrend over the last 10 years

Does this look like an uptrend? It sure does. But perhaps the last 10 years were "special" due to quantitative easing of the Federal Reserve (FED). So, here's the S&P chart for the last 30 years...

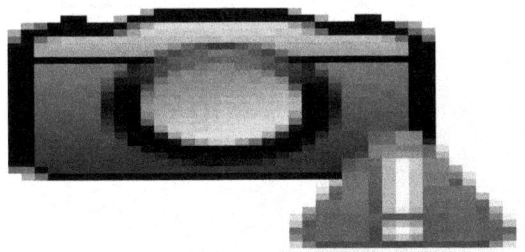

Figure 5.2 – S&P 500 in an uptrend over the last 30 years

It still looks like it's in an uptrend, doesn't it? Now, maybe we got lucky over the last 30 years. So, let's look back further, to the last 70 years...

Figure 5.3 – S&P 500 in an uptrend over the last 70 years

Guess what? The US stock market is still in an uptrend! So, the first thing you need to know is that the US stock market is in a long-term uptrend. This means when you trade stocks, you want to look for buying opportunities and avoid short-selling (not that this doesn't work, but it's much easier to be on the long side than the short). Cool?

2: FOCUS ON STRONG-PERFORMING STOCKS

Let me ask you, what country do you think will win the next World Cup? You'll probably mention countries like Brazil, Germany, France, and Italy, right? That's because these countries have a track record of winning, and they're likely to win again. Some reasons for this could be the availability of talent in these countries, the great training environment, etc. Whatever the case, you can agree that betting on past World Cup winners is a smart choice.

Now you might be wondering, "What does this have to do with trading?" Well, the same concept applies. Strong-performing stocks are likely to perform better than weak ones. This could come down to consistently good earnings, the company being well managed, positive sentiments, and so on. These factors don't just disappear overnight. Rather, they can persist for months or even years—which explains why a stock can trend higher for months or even years.

So the bottom line is this: you want to focus on buying strong-performing stocks—those companies whose stock prices have increased the most over the last 6 to 12 months—because they are likely to continue moving higher.

3: IT'S EASIER TO MAKE MONEY FROM OVERNIGHT TRADING

Overnight trading refers to a trading style in which you hold your trades for at least a day (or more). Some of these trading styles include swing trading and position trading—I'll cover these in more depth later. But for now, the key is to focus on holding positions for at least a day (or more) because it's easier to make money doing this compared to day trading (where you buy/sell your position within the day). So to prove my point, let's run a backtest on the SPY (S&P 500 ETF).

(By the way, I learned this concept from Oddmund Groette, so the credit goes to him.)

Here's how it works…

To simulate day trading, we'll run a backtest from 1993 to 2020. We'll buy the SPY at the open and sell at the close. And we start with an initial capital of $1M. Here's the result…

Net profit: -16.87%

Annual return: -0.66%

Maximum drawdown: -69.11%

Here's the equity curve that represents this…

Figure 5.4 – The result of buying the S&P 500 (SPY) at the open and selling at the close

Now, what if we do the opposite? If we buy at the close and sell at the open, how would the results fare? Here goes...

Net profit: 845.44%

Annual return: 8.35%

Maximum drawdown: 33.84%

Here's the equity curve...

Figure 5.5 – The results of buying the S&P 500 (SPY) at the close and selling at the open

Wow, what a difference! Now, I'm not saying day trading doesn't work because there are traders out there who are doing it successfully. However, if you compare day trading and overnight trading, overnight trading is an easier approach for making money (at least for the US stock market). Does this make sense?

4: SPREAD YOUR BETS

Here's the deal: you can trade in a bull market, identify the strongest stock out there, and have 100% conviction in the stock you're buying. Still, there's a good chance the stock won't perform the way you want it to. For all you know, the stock could quickly reverse and go lower the moment you hit the buy button—and that's the reality of trading. You're dealing with probabilities, never certainties.

Thus, it's important to spread your bets and trade multiple stocks as long as they meet your criteria (instead of going all-in with the "best" stock). This way, the gains from your winners compensate for your losses, and you have a better chance of being profitable in the long run. Let me explain this idea with a few examples…

Scenario 1

- You put all your capital into one stock.
- The stock price drops 30%.
- Net: You're down 30%.

Scenario 2

- You buy 10 different stocks and allocate 10% of your capital to each.
- Four stocks dropped 30%.
- Six stocks increase 30%.
- Net: You are up 6% (calculation: 0.1 [4 × -0.3 + 6 × 0.3] = 0.06).

Does this make sense? Great, then let's move on…

5: KNOW WHEN TO GET OUT

Now, what if you buy a stock and the price immediately moves lower? Do you hold it forever and pray it eventually reverses and goes higher? Of course not, because you never know how low a stock price can go. After all, it could be the next Enron, where the stock goes to zero, and you'll take a big hit to your portfolio (in this scenario, all of your winners combined might not be enough to cover a really big loss).

And that's not all, because your money is also stuck in underperforming stock, and that's an opportunity cost for you. You could allocate those funds to another stock instead of being stuck with a loser. So remember, never marry yourself to a stock. When it's not performing the way you want it to, cut your losses and move on (just like having a fling).

At this point, you've learned the principles of successful stock trading. In the next chapter, you'll discover the three types of trends that most traders are unaware of and how to trade them like a pro.

SUMMARY

- The US stock market is in a long-term uptrend, so wherever possible, look for buying opportunities and avoid short-selling.

- Focus on buying strong-performing stocks because these are the ones that are likely to continue moving higher.

- It's easier to make money holding your positions overnight than day trading.

- Spread your bets across multiple stocks so you can increase your chance of success.

- Never marry yourself to a stock. If it's not working in your favor, cut your losses and move on.

THREE TYPES OF TRENDS
every trader should know

In my early years of trading, I thought an uptrend was simply a series of higher highs and higher lows. Here's what I mean ...

Figure 6.1 – An uptrend

But here's the thing. Sometimes a trend has a shallow pullback, and sometimes it has a deeper one. For example, there have been times when I thought the market was about to make a shallow pullback, but instead, it made a deep pullback—and I'd get stopped out of my trade too early.

Also, there have been times when I thought the market was about to make a deep pullback, and I would patiently wait for it. However, sometimes it seems like the market knows what I'm thinking and makes a slight pullback before rallying higher—causing me to miss the move.

Eventually, I realized not all trends are created equal. That's why you need to understand the different types of trends—so you know how to better time your entries and exits. So the first type of trend is...

1: STRONG TREND

A market is said to be in a strong trend when the price is above the 20-period moving average. In this type of market condition, the pullback is shallow, and the price could find support near the 20-period moving average. Here's an example...

Figure 6.2 – Stock in a strong trend

There are two ways you can trade a strong trend. One way is to buy a breakout when the price breaks above the swing high. Here's what I mean...

Figure 6.3 – Buying a breakout in a strong trending stock

Alternatively, you can go down into a lower timeframe and time your entry on a pullback towards support. Let me give you an example...

Ford is in a strong trend and it made a pullback towards the 20-period moving average on December 3, 2021, as shown below...

Figure 6.4 – Buying a pullback in a strong trending stock (on a lower timeframe)

At this point, you have no idea if there's any buying pressure stepping in to push the price higher. But if you wait for a reversal on the daily timeframe, you could miss a huge chunk of the move. So, what now? In this case, you can go down to the lower timeframe (like the fou-hour) to time your entry. Here's what I mean...

Figure 6.5 – A hammer at support

As you can see, the price came into an area of support and then formed a bullish candlestick pattern (known as a hammer). This is a sign of strength as it signals that buying pressure is stepping in and could push the price higher.

(In the later chapters, I'll dive deeper into support and candlestick patterns. So don't worry if you don't quite understand everything yet. The main takeaway is to understand how you can use multiple timeframes to time your entry in a strong trend. Cool?)

2: HEALTHY TREND

A market is said to be in a healthy trend when the price is above the 50-period moving average. In this type of market condition, the pullback is healthy (and deeper than a strong trend), and the price could find support near the 50-period moving average. Here's an example…

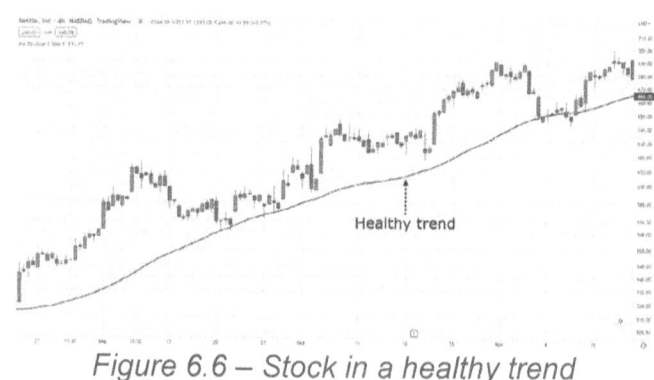

Figure 6.6 – Stock in a healthy trend

In a healthy trend, you can enter on a pullback as the price approaches the 50-period moving average. Often, you'll also notice the 50-period moving average coincides with previous resistance that could become support, and this makes this setup even more attractive. Here's what I mean…

Figure 6.7 – Previous resistance becomes support

But what about trading a breakout? Should you buy a breakout when the market is in a healthy trend? Well, you can, but you require a larger stop loss because the price could make a pullback towards the 50-period moving average after you buy the breakout. So, to avoid getting stopped out prematurely, you need a larger stop loss in order to withstand the pullback that could occur.

(In a later chapter, I'll teach you more about stop loss and how to set a proper one. So don't worry if this doesn't make sense yet.)

3: WEAK TREND

A market is said to be in a weak trend when the price is above the 200-period moving average. In this kind of market condition, the pullback is weak (and it's deeper than a healthy trend), and the price could find support near the 100- or 200-period moving average. Here's an example…

Figure 6.8 – A weak trend

In a weak trend, you can enter on a pullback as the price approaches the 100- or 200-period moving average.

This usually coincides with an area of support. Here's what I mean...

Figure 6.9 – Price makes a pullback towards support

At this point, you've learned about the three types of trends and how to trade them accordingly. Next, you'll discover specific entry triggers you can use to time your entry.

SUMMARY

- A strong trend occurs when the price is above the 20-period moving average. The pullback is shallow, and the price could find support near the 20-period moving average.

- A healthy trend occurs when the price is above the 50-period moving average. The pullback is healthy, and the price could find support near the 50-period moving average.

- A weak trend occurs when the price is above the 200-period moving average. The pullback is deep, and the price could find support at the 100- or 200-period moving average.

AREA OF VALUE: HOW TO BUY LOW and sell high

Let me ask you how much you'd pay for an apple (note: this is not a trick question). I'm guessing you wouldn't pay more than $1 because you know the value of an apple. After visiting a few supermarkets (or grocery stores), you'll have an idea of how much an apple costs, and whether you're overpaying for one.

However, when it comes to stock trading, how do you know whether the stock price you're paying is overvalued or undervalued? Unlike apples, which are sold in different supermarkets, there's no benchmark you can use to compare the price against. Well, this is where the concept of area of value comes into play.

AREA OF VALUE

Area of value refers to an area on your chart where buying pressure could step in and push the price higher. There are a number of ways to define an area of value:

- Support and resistance
- Trendline
- Moving average

Let's look at these concepts in more detail...

SUPPORT AND RESISTANCE EXPLAINED

Support is a horizontal area on your chart where buying pressure could step in and push the price higher. Here's what it looks like...

Figure 7.1 – An area of support

Now, you might be thinking, "Why does support work?" Support works because the market is watched by traders all over the world. If they notice the price has repeatedly reversed higher at a certain level, they'll think it's likely this could happen again.

So what do traders do? They buy at support, hoping to make a profit. And if enough traders do this, it becomes a self-fulfilling prophecy, and support ends up becoming support.

Now, the opposite of support is resistance. Resistance is a horizontal area on your chart where selling pressure could step in and push the price lower. Here's what it looks like...

Figure 7.2 – An area of resistance

WHEN THE PRICE BREAKS SUPPORT, IT COULD BECOME RESISTANCE

As you know, support is an area where buying pressure could step in and push the price higher. The keyword here is *could*. This means there's no guarantee that the price will bounce off support. It could just as well break below support. When this happens, the area of support could now become resistance. Here's what I mean...

Figure 7.3 – Previous support becomes resistance

But why does this happen? The theory behind it is this: when the price comes into support, a group of traders will go long, thinking the market is about to reverse higher. Now, imagine that the price breaks through support; this group of traders is now sitting on losses, hoping the market will move back in their favor.

Now, what if the market decides to give them a chance, and it moves higher back towards their entry point? How would the traders feel? Relieved! What was previously a huge loss is now a golden opportunity to exit their trade at breakeven—and so, they do just that.

Now, to exit a long trade you need to sell your position. And when many traders do this, it creates selling pressure in the market, and that's how previous support could become resistance.

Likewise, when the price breaks above resistance, it could become support. Here's an example...

Figure 7.4 – Previous resistance becomes support

At this point, you're starting to understand what support and resistance are. But now the question is, how do you draw them accurately? Well, it's difficult to explain this with text. That's why I've included a bonus training that explains how to do it step-by-step. Here's the link: bonus.stocktradingbook.com

TRENDLINE EXPLAINED

The concept of a trendline is similar to support and resistance. The difference is, instead of being presented as horizontal, a trendline is drawn diagonally on your chart. Here's what I mean...

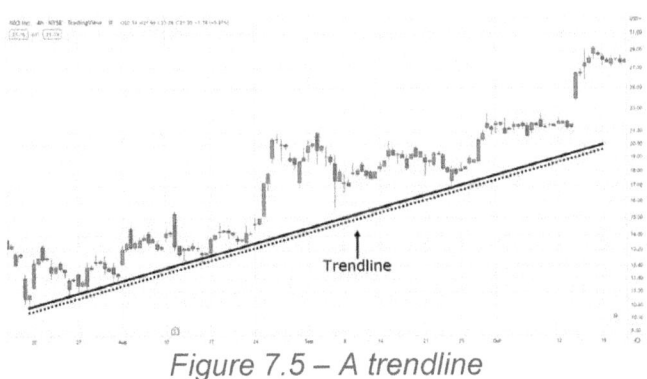

Figure 7.5 – A trendline

Now to confirm the validity of a trendline, there's at least two tests you can do to connect the swing points. Here's an example...

Figure 7.6 – Two touches of a trendline

Now you're probably wondering, "How do I use the area of value concept in my trading?" Simple. If you identify a stock in an uptrend, you can wait for it to retrace towards an area of value (like support or a trendline) to time your entry. This way, you won't be chasing the market but rather trading from an area where buying pressure could step in and push the price higher. Does this make sense? Great! Now, let me share with you another way to define an area of value using an indicator…

MOVING AVERAGE EXPLAINED

The moving average indicator calculates the average price over a given period. So for a 5-day moving average, it calculates the average price over the last 5 days. For a 10-day moving average, it calculates the average price over the last 10 days. Clear?

For this explanation, I'll use the 10-day moving average as an example. Here's what it looks like...

Figure 7.7 – 10-day moving average

So, how does the 10-day moving average work? Let me explain...

Imagine Stock ABC has the following closing prices over the last 10 days: $1, $2, $3, $4, $5, $6, $7, $8, $9, $10.

So, what's the average price over the last 10 days? Well, you need to add the prices over the last 10 days and divide by 10. This gives you [1 + 2 + 3 + 4 + 5 + 6 + 7 + 8 + 9 + 10] / 10 = 5.5.

This means the 10-day moving average value is 5.5.

Now, if stock ABC closes at $20 on the 11th day, what's the 10-day moving average? Again, we'll add the 10 *most recent* closing prices and divide them by 10. This gives you…

[2 + 3 + 4 + 5 + 6 + 7 + 8 + 9 + 10 + 20] / 10 = 7.4.

This means the 10-day moving average value is 7.4.

Now, you might be wondering, "How does the 10-day moving average becomes a line on the chart?"

Well, a 10-day moving average value will show up as a "dot" on the chart. As new prices are formed, the 10-day moving average is recalculated and will show up as a new "dot" on the chart. When you connect the "dots," it becomes a line on your chart.

Now that you understand what the moving average is, let's learn how you can use it to identify the area of value…

HOW TO USE MOVING AVERAGE TO IDENTIFY THE AREA OF VALUE

Here are two general rules to use to identify the area of value when the market is trending.

1. The stock has bounced off the 50-period moving average at least twice.

Here's an example…

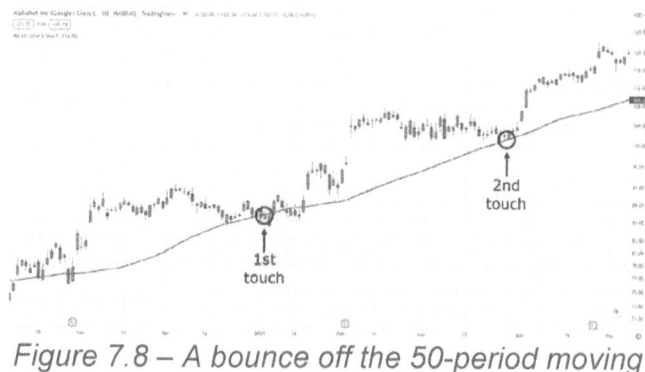

Figure 7.8 – A bounce off the 50-period moving average

As you can see, the price bounced off the 50-period moving average twice. So, when the price retests a third time, we can reference the 50-period moving average as an area of value where you can look for buying opportunities.

Now, there's nothing magical about the 50-period moving average. You can use other parameters like the 20-period moving average or even the 100-period moving average. The reason I use the 50-period moving average is that it allows me to identify the area of value when the market is trending in a 45-degree manner (i.e., the angle of the moving average is at a 45-degree angle)—which is the type of trend I prefer to trade.

STACKED AREA OF VALUE

This refers to multiple areas of value that overlap one another. This is powerful because it gathers the interest of more traders—which makes a reversal more likely. For example, you can have the price approaching the 50-period moving average, which coincides with an area of support. Here's what I mean…

Figure 7.9 – The 50-period moving average coincides with an area of support

And that's not all, because you can also combine support with a trendline. Here's what I mean…

Figure 7.10 – The trendline coincides with an area of support

So whenever you spot a stacked area of value, pay close attention because there's a good chance the stock could reverse higher from there.

At this point, you've learned how to identify an area of value using tools like support and resistance, trendline, and moving average. The next thing to look for is a valid entry trigger to tell you when exactly to enter a trade. And that's what I'll cover next…

SUMMARY

- Area of value helps you pinpoint where buying (or selling) pressure could step in and push the price higher (or lower).

- Support is an area where buying pressure could step in and push the price higher. Resistance is an area where selling pressure could step in and push the price lower.

- The concept of a trendline is similar to support and resistance. The difference is, it's drawn as a diagonal line instead of a horizontal.

- When the price breaks below support, it could become resistance. When the price breaks above resistance, it could become support.

- In a 45-degree trend, you can

use the 50-period moving average to identify an area of value.

- When multiple areas of value coincide, it increases the odds of a reversal in that area.

ENTRY TRIGGERS: PRICE PATTERNS TO BETTER TIME
your entry

I had a crush on a girl when I was 17 years old. We met at camp. She had fair skin, shoulder-length brown hair, and big round eyes.

I told myself: "That's a girl I'd love to be with for the rest of my life!" So what did I do? Well, I chased her, of course.

Now, I had no tactics, no game plan, or anything like that. But hey, I had watched a ton of romantic movies.

What I noticed in these movies was that happy endings always occurred when the guy was being sweet—that was my "aha" moment! Just be nice = win the girl.

At this point, I had her number on my contact list. So here's what I did. I messaged her three to four times a week. And I asked her things like

- "What are you doing now?"
- "Any plans for the weekend?"
- "Do you want to meet up?"

After six months, I couldn't take it anymore. I had to confess my feelings because it seemed like my heart was going to explode!

So one day, I asked her to meet up with me because I had something to tell her. And guess what? She said she had something to tell me too. *OMG! Did she feel the same way about me?!*

So, we met up. And she started the ball rolling by confessing she had feelings— for my friend.

I was dazed for a moment, and felt the world spinning around me. For the rest of the night, I listened to her talk about how much she liked this other guy and ask questions about what she should do.

That night, I went home feeling squashed. My breathing was heavy, my eyes were teary, and my heart was filled with gloom. It hurts.

Did I survive? You bet. If not, I wouldn't be writing this now, LOL. Anyway moving on…

I was 23 years old and I had another crush on a girl during my first year at university. And of course, I chased her.

However, I recalled my previous failure and attributed it to not doing enough. So, what did I do this time around? Well, I upped the ante! I did even more.

I texted her five times a week. I initiated conversations all the time. I wrote long messages in the hopes of offering her something to reply to.

And after three months, I confessed that I liked her—and got rejected, again. *Ouch! I felt like a failure and that perhaps I was meant to be alone in this world.*

Me being me, I moved on. So on to girl number three...

I was in my final year and about to take my last exam. (In other words, after this day, I'd never see many of my schoolmates again.)

Here's what happened that day. I was waiting to board a train to my exam hall. While waiting, I bumped into a familiar-looking girl (let's call her Mary).

I'd seen Mary around because she was the type of student who always asked questions in class. She was sweet-looking, and she had long black hair and smooth skin.

Now, I didn't know her personally, but we were both kind of aware of each other's existence. I figured I'd probably never see her again, so I asked her for her mobile number. And surprisingly, Mary gave it to me!

If you recall, my previous two attempts failed when I was showing a ton of care and concern for the girl. So this time around, I did the complete opposite. Instead of texting long messages, I replied less than she did. Instead of initiating a conversation, I waited for her to initiate one first. Instead of replying immediately, I'd wait for hours or even days to reply.

After going back and forth for three months, we got together! *It worked! I had a girlfriend! I felt loved and accepted!*

So what I've learned is this: When going after girls, less is more. Don't be available all the time. Don't give them attention. Do as little as possible. Why? Because less is more!

Now you're wondering, "Why am I sharing this story with you?" Because the same can be said for trading—less is more.

So when it comes to entry triggers, you don't need to know all the different types of price patterns. Instead, you just need to know whether a stock is making a pullback or a breakout. Then you can adopt the right entry trigger to enter a trade. Let me explain…

Pullback

A pullback occurs when the price makes a retracement (or a move) against the trend. Here's what I mean…

Figure 8.1 – A pullback

Advantage: It's psychologically easier because you are buying low and selling higher.

Disadvantage: In a strongly trending market, the pullback might not reach your level, and you'll end up missing the move.

Next…

Breakout

A breakout occurs when the price moves beyond a certain "boundary" (like a swing high or resistance). Here's what I mean…

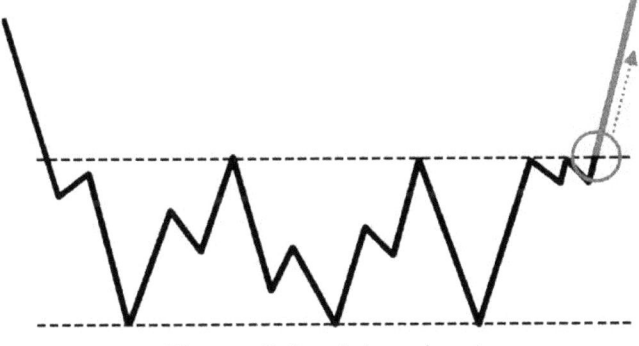

Figure 8.2 – A breakout

Advantage: You get more trading opportunities.

Disadvantage: It might be psychologically difficult because you are buying high and selling higher.

Next, let's dive into specific entry triggers so you'll understand when exactly to enter a trade. To get started, I'd like to give you an introduction to candlestick patterns…

CANDLESTICK PATTERNS EXPLAINED

A candlestick pattern has four data points:

Open: the opening price

High: the highest price over a specific time period

Low: the lowest price over a specific time period

Close: the closing price

Here's what this looks like…

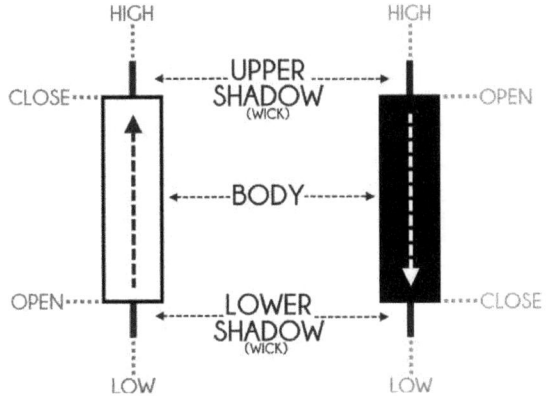

Figure 8.3 – Candlestick patterns explained

Now, a candlestick pattern can be formed across different timeframes, like daily, weekly, monthly, etc. So if you're on the daily timeframe, this means a new candlestick will be formed every day. If you're on the weekly timeframe, then a new candle is formed every week. Does this make sense?

If so, let's move on and learn about bullish reversal candlestick patterns because you can use these to time your entry in a healthy or a weak trend...

BULLISH REVERSAL CANDLESTICK PATTERNS

A bullish reversal candlestick pattern signifies that buyers are momentarily in control. When this pattern is formed, you can enter the trade on the next candle's open (after taking into account the market structure and area of value).

Now, bullish reversal candlestick patterns can be expressed in many ways, and it's not within the scope of this book to cover them all. But here are two useful ones to get you started…

- Hammer
- Bullish engulfing pattern

Hammer

A hammer is a (one-candle) bullish reversal pattern that forms after a price decline.

Here's how to recognize one…

1. There's little or no upper shadow.
2. The price closes at the top ¼ of

the range.
3. The lower shadow is about two or three times the length of the body.

Here's an example…

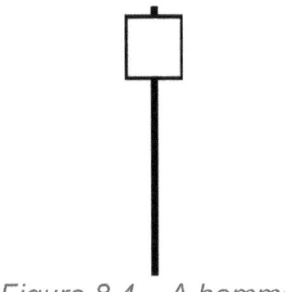

Figure 8.4 – A hammer

And this is what a hammer means:

- When the market opened, the sellers took control and pushed the price lower.
- At the selling climax, huge buying pressure stepped in, which pushed the price higher.
- The buying pressure was so strong that it closed above the opening price.

In short, a hammer is a bullish reversal candlestick pattern that shows rejection of lower prices. So, if you use the hammer as an entry trigger, you can enter at the open of the next candle.

Bullish engulfing pattern

A bullish engulfing pattern is a (two-candle) bullish reversal pattern that forms after a price decline.

Here's how to recognize one…

1. The first candle has a bearish close.
2. On the second candle, the market gaps below the low of the first candle and then closes above the high of the first candle.
3. The second candle closes bullish.

Here's an example…

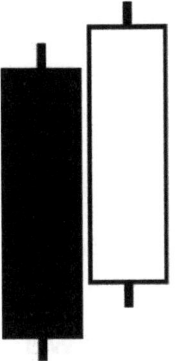

Figure 8.5 – A bullish engulfing pattern

And this is what a bullish engulfing pattern means:

- On the first candle, the sellers are in control because they closed lower for the period.
- On the second candle, strong buying pressure stepped in, and the close was above the previous candle's high, which tells you that the buyers have won the battle for now.

In essence, a bullish engulfing pattern tells you that the buyers have overwhelmed the sellers and they're now in control. So, if you use the bullish engulfing pattern as an entry trigger, you can enter at the open of the next candle.

Now, what about bearish reversal candlestick patterns? I won't go into details because you want to look for buying opportunities in the stock market. Anyway, it's not hard to figure this out because it's simply the opposite of bullish reversal candlestick patterns.

Moving on, let's learn about the false break, which you can use to time your entry on a pullback...

FALSE BREAK

The false break occurs when the price trades below support (or a swing low) before it quickly reverses higher (also known as a false breakout).

Here's how to recognize a false break…

1. The price makes a move into support or a swing low.

2. It trades below support and quickly reverses higher.
3. Finally, the price closes back above support.

Here's an example...

Figure 8.6 – A false break

Now, why would you want to use this as an entry trigger? There are two reasons for this...

(The explanation below can be used for bullish candlestick patterns too.)

A sign of strength

When the price breaks below support, it puts selling pressure in the market from traders exiting their long positions (as it hits their stop loss) and bearish traders who short the breakdown of support. However, if the price didn't go lower but instead rallied higher back above support, what would that tell you? It's a sign of strength because buying pressure is stepping in to push the price higher.

Lower risk

A false break allows you to enter a trade with lower risk. That's because you can place your stop loss below the recent low that was formed—this offers you a more favorable risk to reward on your trade.

You might be wondering, "Are there any specific price patterns to look for in the false break?" The key is to look for the price making a swift reversal above support. Visually, it looks like a big bullish candle closing back above support. This could be in the form of a hammer or a bullish engulfing pattern, and sometimes there's no name for the pattern. Here's an example...

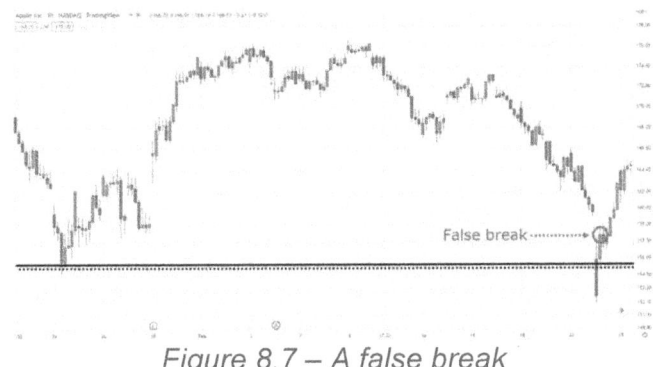

Figure 8.7 – A false break

Next, let's learn which entry triggers to trade during a breakout...

BREAKOUT WITH A BUILDUP

When trading breakouts, you want to avoid buying when the stock has recently made a big move—the type of move where the stock price just keeps going higher over the last 5 to 10 candles. Why? This is because the market is likely to be "exhausted" and about to make a pullback or a reversal.

Instead, you want to look to trade a breakout with a buildup. Now you're probably wondering, "What's a buildup?" A buildup is a tight consolidation, and you'll notice the range of the candles is small in the consolidation.

Here's how to recognize one...

1. The price is stuck in a range between support and resistance.
2. Then it approaches resistance and consolidates at that area.
3. You'll notice the range of the candles is getting smaller.

Here's an example...

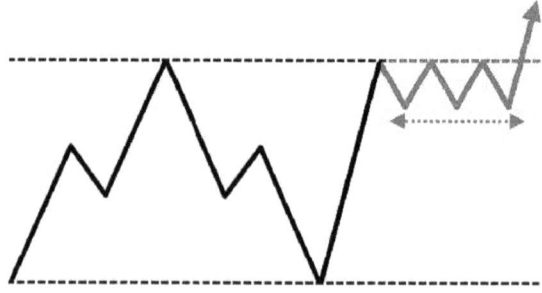

Figure 8.8 – A breakout with a buildup

Now you might be thinking, "Why trade a breakout with a buildup?" There are two reasons for this…

Lower risk

If you "chase" breakouts or enter after the market has made a huge move higher, then you'll need a large stop loss. That's because the nearest place to set your stop loss is below the previous swing low or support—and that's usually far from your entry price.

However, if you trade a breakout with a buildup, then you can reference the low of the buildup to set your stop loss. This means your stop loss will be tighter, and you'll get a more favorable risk to reward on your trade. (I'll talk more about setting a stop loss in a later chapter.)

Better odds

Here's the thing. The market moves from a period of low volatility to high volatility and vice versa. Here's what I mean…

Figure 8.9 – *The market moves from a period of low volatility to a period of high volatility (and vice versa)*

In layman's terms, if the market is quiet (low volatility), then it's likely to make a big move soon. In contrast, if the market is noisy (high volatility), then things could get quiet soon.

So when you trade a breakout with a buildup, you're entering a trade when the market is quiet—just when something big is about to happen. Now you might be thinking, "How many candles must the buildup be?"

Now, there's no fixed rule to this. But a guideline you can use is to wait for the 20-period moving average to touch the low of the buildup. When that happens, it's a signal the market has stored enough "energy" to make the next run higher. Here's what I mean…

Figure 8.10 – The 20-period moving average touches the low of the buildup

So if you want to trade the breakout with a buildup, you can enter when the price breaks above the high of the buildup (using a buy stop order or waiting for a close above the level).

Now another variation of this entry trigger is the bull flag pattern…

BULL FLAG

A bull flag is a trend continuation chart pattern that signals the market is likely to continue higher.

Here's how to recognize it…

1. The market is in an uptrend (or has recently broken above resistance).
2. The market then makes a pullback that doesn't exceed the 20-period moving average.
3. You'll notice the range of the candles is smaller compared to the earlier trending move.

Here's an example…

Figure 8.11 – A bull flag pattern

For the bull flag pattern, you can enter when the price breaks above the high of the bull flag pattern (using a buy stop order or waiting for a close above the level).

As you can see, the bull flag pattern is like a breakout with a buildup. The only difference is that, for a bull flag pattern, the market is already trending high, whereas in the case of breakout with a buildup, the market is in a range.

At this point, you've learned different entry triggers so you can time your entry on a pullback or a breakout. Next, you'll discover how to exit your trades when the market moves in your favor or against you.

SUMMARY

- An entry trigger is a specific price pattern that tells you when exactly to enter a trade.

- To trade a pullback, you can use entry triggers like bullish reversal candlestick patterns or a false break pattern.

- To trade a breakout, you can use entry triggers like the breakout with a buildup or a bull flag pattern.

EXITS: HOW TO PROTECT YOUR DOWNSIDE and maximize your profits

As you've just discovered, I'm a slow learner when it comes to chasing girls. Thus, I don't have many exits to speak of. Fortunately, we're not talking about relationships here but trading exits, a topic I have a lot more to share on. So when it comes to exits, there are two things to consider:

- Stop loss: when do you sell if the market moves against you?
- Target profit: when do you sell if the market moves in your favor?

Let's begin with your stop loss...

STOP LOSS

A stop loss protects your downside. It answers the question "Where do you exit the trade if the market goes against you?" As a general rule, you want to exit your trade when your trading setup is invalidated.

For example, if a stock is in a healthy trend, and you want to buy at support, then it makes sense to have your stop loss below support. That's because when you buy at support, you expect the price to move higher. But if it breaks below support, then it's likely the market isn't behaving the way you expect, and you should exit the trade to minimize your losses.

Now, you don't want to place your stop loss one tick below support because the market could easily swing lower, take out your stop loss, then reverse higher. Another reason is that support is an area on your chart, not a specific line.

This means even if the market breaks one tick below support, support isn't necessarily broken because the market could be retracing deeper into support.

So where am I going with this? Well, you want to set your stop loss some distance from price structure (in this case, support). This way, your trade has more "breathing room," and it stands less of a chance of being stopped out by random fluctuations of the market. Here's how to set up your stop loss:

1. Identify the price structure (in this case, the low of support).
2. Find the current average true (ATR) value.
3. Subtract 1 ATR from the low of support.

You might be wondering, "What's the average true range?" This trading indicator calculates the historical volatility of the market. In other words, it tells you how much the market has moved on average over a given period. For example, if you use a 20-period ATR, then it calculates the average volatility of the market over the last 20 days.

Once you know the current ATR value (which is shown on the indicator), you simply subtract it from the low of support—and that's your stop loss. Here's what I mean…

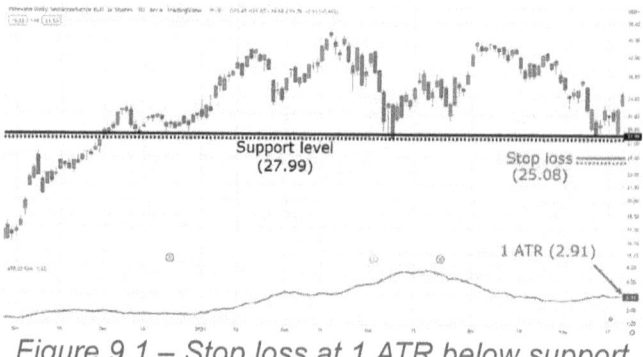

Figure 9.1 – Stop loss at 1 ATR below support

As you can see, the ATR value acts as an extra buffer for your stop loss. This means the market has to break below support by a bigger margin before you're stopped out. Of course, you'll still get stopped out of your trade from time to time. But when you do get stopped out, you want this to happen because support has broken and not because your stop loss is too tight.

Let's look at another example. Let's say your trading setup is to buy a breakout. In this case, it makes sense to have your stop loss below the breakout point. That's because, when you buy a breakout, you expect the price to quickly move higher. But if it reverses instead, and the price drops below the breakout point, then it's likely the breakout has failed and you'll want to exit your trade.

But where exactly do you set your stop loss? Again, the same concept applies:

1. Identify the price structure (in this case, the breakout point).
2. Find the current ATR value.
3. Subtract 1 ATR from the breakout point.

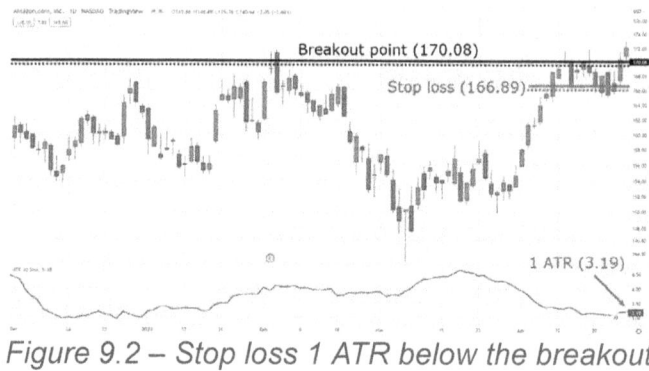

Figure 9.2 – Stop loss 1 ATR below the breakout point

As you can see, when the price breaks out of resistance, this is where previous resistance could now become support. The last thing you want to do is exit your trade at support because this is an area where buying pressure could step in and push the price higher.

Instead, you want to set your stop loss 1 ATR below the breakout point. This way, if the price reaches your stop loss, it's a sign that support has broken, and you'll want to get out of your losing trade. Next, let's move on and learn how to exit your winning trades…

TAKE PROFIT

When it comes to taking profits, there are two approaches you can consider:

1. Swing trading: capturing a swing
2. Trend following: riding a trend

Let me explain further…

Swing trading

If you hear the term swing trading, this refers to a trading style that seeks to capture a swing in the market (in other words, to capture one move).

The idea behind this is to exit your trade before opposing pressure steps in. For example, if you bought near the low of support (in a healthy trend), then you want to exit your trade before resistance—where selling pressure might step in. Here's an example…

Figure 9.3 – Take profit before the nearest swing high

Let's assume you bought Marvell at $82. Now, if you want to capture a swing, then the swing high near $92 is the level at which you'll want to exit your trade because that's where selling pressure might step in.

Pros: If you set a proper target profit, you can expect a higher winning rate compared to adopting a trend-following approach.

Cons: You won't be able to ride trends.

Now, if riding a trend is something you're interested in doing, then the next approach is for you...

Trend following

If you want to ride a trend, you can't have a target profit. That's because a target profit gets you out of a trade. And if you exited your position, how do you ride a trend when you've got nothing left?

If you want to ride a trend, the key is to use a trailing stop loss. For example, if the market is trending higher, you'll shift your stop loss progressively higher—and you'll only exit the trade if the market hits your stop loss.

For instance, you can use a percentage change in price as a trailing stop loss. This means you'll exit your position only if the price closes X% below your entry price.

To illustrate this, let's say you buy a breakout on Ford and you want to use a 20% trailing stop loss. Here's what I mean…

Figure 9.4 – A trailing stop loss

As you can see, Ford broke out higher and closed at $21.45. Now, let's say you enter at the next day's open at $21.45, and you intend to use a 20% trailing stop loss. This means your initial stop loss is at $17.16 (calculation: $21.45 × 0.8 = $17.16).

What if the price of Ford reaches $30? Where would your trailing stop loss be? It would be at $24 (calculation $30 × 0.8 = $24). Clearly, as the price moves higher, so will your trailing stop loss. And you'll remain in the trade until the price hits your trailing stop loss.

Also, the 20% trailing stop loss isn't fixed because you can adjust it to suit your needs. For example, if you want to ride a short-term trend, you can use a 10% trailing stop loss. Or if you want to ride a longer-term trend, you can trail with a 40% trailing stop loss.

Pros: Your profits are larger than your losses.

Cons: You have a lower winning rate.

Now, a percentage drop in price isn't the only technique you can use to trail your stop loss. You can also use things like price structure, the chandelier exit, etc.

You can learn more in the bonus training that comes with this book. Here's the link: bonus.stocktradingbook.com

HYBRID APPROACH

This method combines capturing a swing and riding a trend. The idea is to exit a portion of your position at a fixed target, and then to have the remaining position use a trailing stop loss to ride the trend. Here's what I mean...

Figure 9.5 – A hybrid approach between taking profits and trailing your stop loss

As a general rule, you can exit 50% of your position at a fixed target and trail your stop loss on the remaining position. Of course, you can adjust this higher or lower depending on your goals—there's no right or wrong here.

Pros: You can capture a swing and still ride a trend.

Cons: If you do catch a trend, your profit is smaller because you've exited some of your position.

At this point, you've learned how to exit your trades when the market moves against you or in your favor. Next, I'll cover some powerful risk management techniques you can adopt so you'll never blow up another trading account.

SUMMARY

- Your stop loss should be at a level that invalidates your trading setup.

- To capture a swing, you want to exit your trade before opposing pressure steps in.

- To ride a trend, you want to exit your trade only when your trailing stop loss is hit.

- Hybrid approach: You can sell 50% of your position at a fixed target and trail the remaining half of your position to ride a trend.

RISK MANAGEMENT and position sizing

Back in my proprietary trading days, I knew of a trader called John (not his real name). I recall one particular day when John was down $300,000 after a few hours of trading. His boss told him to take a break and stop trading for the day. However, John didn't cave. He wanted to continue fighting until the end of the session, and so he did.

At the end of the day, John managed to recover his losses and was back at breakeven. Still, he needed to pay commissions regardless of whether he made or lost money. Can you guess how much John paid in commissions that day? A whopping $50,000! In other words, he lost $50,000 that day despite having a breakeven day. And with this trading approach, John made $1M for that year.

Now, fast forward to today. Can you guess how much money John is making? Nothing, zero, zilch. He left the trading industry because he eventually returned all the profits he had made in the earlier years, and more. The reason I'm sharing this story is to highlight the importance of risk management and position sizing. Let me explain further...

Imagine two traders, John and Sally.

- John and Sally both have $10,000 trading accounts.
- They use the same trading strategy, which has a 50% winning rate and a 1:2 risk-to-reward ratio. (Risk-to-reward ratio refers to how much you earn relative to the amount you risk. If you risk $100 on a trade and earn $300, that's a risk-to-reward ratio of 1 to 3.)

- John risks $2,500 on each trade.
- Sally risks $200 on each trade.

The outcome of their next 10 trades is as follows: *Lose, Lose, Lose, Lose, Win, Lose, Win, Win, Win, Win*

So what's the outcome for both traders?

John: -$2,500, -$2,500, -$2,500, -$2,500 = -$10,000

Sally: -$200, -$200, -$200, -$200, +$400, -$200, +$400, +$400, +$400, +$400 = $1,000

As you can see, both John and Sally used the same trading strategy but with different outcomes.

John lost his entire account because he risked too much on each trade. After four losing trades in a row, he wiped out his account.

Sally, on the other hand, risked a small amount on each trade, and she managed to ride out the drawdown. In the end, she made a profit of $1,000—which is a 10% gain on her account.

Can you see the importance of risk management? Without it, even the best trading strategy won't help you become a profitable trader.

The next question is, how do you apply proper risk management? And that's what I'll cover next…

POSITION SIZING EXPLAINED

Position sizing allows you to trade with the correct number of shares so that even if a trade is a loser, the loss is only a fraction of your trading account.

As a general rule, a loss shouldn't cost you more than 1% of your account. For example, if your account is $10,000, then a loss shouldn't be more than $100 (calculation: 0.01 x $10,000 = $100). This way, even if you encounter 10 losses in a row, you're still left with

90% of your capital, which is a manageable position to recover from.

So how do you know how many shares to trade to ensure your loss is only 1% of your capital? Here's the formula...

Position size = Amount to risk in $ / Distance of your stop loss in $

The distance of your stop loss in $ is determined by two things:

1. Entry price
2. Stop loss price

So if your entry price is $20 and your stop loss price is $17, this means the distance of your stop loss is $3 (calculation: $20 - $17 = $3). Now, let's have a look at an example so it all makes sense...

Example 1

- You want to buy Apple stock.
- The amount to risk on this trade

is $100.
- The distance of your stop loss is $5.

How many shares of Apple can you buy so you only lose $100 if the market hits your stop loss?

Using the formula...

Position size = $ Amount to risk / $ amount of your stop loss

Position size = $100 / $5

Position size = 20 shares of Apple

This means you can buy 20 shares of Apple, and if the price of Apple drops by $5, you'll lose $100 on the trade. Here's another example...

Example 2

- You want to buy Walt Disney stock.
- The amount to risk on this trade is $500.

- The distance of your stop loss is $0.5.

How many shares of Walt Disney stock should you buy?

Again, using the formula…

Position size = $ Amount to risk / $ amount of your stop loss

Position size = $500 / $0.5

Position size = 1,000 shares of Walt Disney stock

This means you can buy 1,000 shares of Walt Disney stock, and if the price of Walt Disney drops by $0.5, you'll lose $500 on the trade. And one last example…

Example 3

- You want to buy Goldman Sachs stock.
- The amount to risk on this trade is $50.

- The distance of your stop loss is $100.

How many shares of Goldman Sachs stock should you buy? Well, if you're using this trading setup, it isn't possible to buy any shares of Goldman Sachs because the distance of your stop loss is larger than the amount you're willing to risk on the trade.

Even if you buy one share of Goldman Sachs, that's a potential loss of $100—which is higher than the $50 that you're willing to risk on this trade. Does this make sense?

And by the way, you don't have to calculate your position size manually because you can use a position sizing calculator. I've included one in the bonus resources that come with this book, and you can find it here: bonus.stocktradingbook.com

At this point, you've learned the importance of risk management and how to calculate your optimal position size according to your risk profile. Next, you'll discover how to assess your risk-to-reward ratio in trading and learn how to use it to your advantage.

SUMMARY

- Proper risk management allows you to weather a series of losses without blowing up your trading account.

- Applying proper risk management means trading with the correct position size.

- Position size = Amount to risk in $ / Distance of your stop loss in $.

THE TRUTH ABOUT risk-to-reward ratio

I started my trading career back in 2010. At that time, there wasn't a lot of freely available information, so I browsed trading forums, blogs, and books to learn as much as I could.

One thing I noticed people preaching was that if you wanted to be a profitable trader, you had to have a minimum risk-to-reward ratio of 1:2. The logic behind this argument was that if your winners were larger than your losers, you could win less than 50% of the time and still be a profitable trader.

Initially, this made a lot of sense to me. But as I dug deeper, I realized that your risk-to-reward ratio alone doesn't give you the full picture—and it can even be misleading. I'll explain more in this chapter, but first, let's start with the basics, so we're on the same page…

Risk-to-reward ratio is a term used by traders to measure your risk relative to your return. Here's what I mean…

Example 1

- You risk $100 on the trade.
- You make $300 on the trade.

So what's the risk to reward on this trade? Well, it's a risk-to-reward ratio of 1:3. In other words, you made $3 for every $1 you risked on this trade.

Example 2

- You risk $500 on the trade.
- You make $250 on the trade.

In this case, you're working with a 1:0.5 risk-to-reward ratio. This means you made $0.5 for every $1 you risked on this trade.

(Another similar concept is called the R multiple, popularized by Dr. Van K. Tharp. Here's how it works: Instead of saying you achieved a one-to-three risk-to-reward ratio, you could say you had a gain of 3R. This means you made three times the amount you risked, or $3 for every $1 you risked.)

Now you might be thinking, "Easy! All I need to do is to identify trades with favorable risk-to-reward ratios (like 1:3 or more), and I can be a profitable trader." Well, not so fast, because the risk-to-reward ratio is only one side of the equation. The other is your winning rate. Here's what I mean…

Example 3

- Let's say you risk $100 on a trade.
- You have a target of $500.

- This means you have a potential risk-to-reward ratio of 1:5.

Now, what if you only win 10% of the time? Clearly, even with a 1:5 risk-to-reward ratio, you'll remain a loser in the long run.

So, what's the lesson? On its own, your risk-to-reward ratio or winning rate is meaningless—it doesn't tell you whether your trading strategy will make money in the long run or not.

But when you combine your risk-to-reward ratio with your winning rate, and you have a positive expectancy (otherwise known as an edge), you'll know if you have what it takes to become a consistently profitable trader. So here's the formula for expectancy:

Expectancy = (average gain x probability of gain) - (average loss x probability of loss)

Here's an example:

Example 4

- Your winning rate is 50%.
- Your losing rate is 50%.
- The average size of your gain is $500.
- The average size of your loss is $300.

So what's your expectancy?

Well, using the formula...

Expectancy = (average gain x probability of gain) - (average loss x probability of loss)

Expectancy = ($500 × 50%) - ($300 × 50%)

Expectancy = $100

Now, how do you interpret this number? Simple—it means you can expect to make an average of $100 per trade.

So if a trader executes 100 trades, he can expect to make about $10,000 (calculation: $100 × 100 = $10,000).

As you can see, you can have a positive expectancy even though you only win 50% of the time because of your favorable risk-to-reward ratio. Here's another example…

Example 5

- Your winning rate is 20%.
- Your losing rate is 80%.
- The average size of your gain is $500.
- The average size of your loss is $300.

Now, what's your expectancy?

Again, using the formula…

Expectancy = (average gain x probability of gain) - (average loss x probability of loss)

Expectancy = ($500 × 20%) - ($300 × 80%)

Expectancy = -$140

In this case, you have a negative expectancy of -$140. This means that in the long run, you can expect to lose an average of $140 per trade. So after 100 trades, you can expect to lose around $14,000.

But wait, didn't you have a favorable risk-to-reward ratio? Yes. But remember, your risk-to-reward ratio is meaningless on its own. Instead, you must combine it with your winning rate to know whether you'll make money in the long run or not.

That being said, if you can consistently get favorable risk-to-reward trading opportunities, then you don't need a high winning rate to be a profitable trader. So now the question is...

HOW DO YOU IDENTIFY FAVORABLE RISK-TO-REWARD TRADING SETUPS?

There are a few things you can do, so let's analyze them one by one…

Reduce your stop loss

If you reduce the size of your stop loss, it's easier to achieve a favorable risk to reward on your trades. For example, if your stop loss is $1 and the stock moves $3 in your favor, then that's a 1:3 risk-to-reward ratio (or a gain of 3R).

However, a $1 stop loss is usually too tight for most stocks (especially if you trade on a higher timeframe, like the daily). This means you'll likely get stopped out before the price reaches your target. So yes, a smaller stop loss will improve your risk to reward on the trade, but you can't blindly set one up because you'll get stopped out by the slightest noise in the market (which will reduce your winning rate). Next…

Increase your target profit

Now, you can also increase your target profit and thereby improve your risk to reward on the trade. For example, if you have a stop loss of $10 and a target profit of $100, that's a potential risk to reward of 1:10.

However, if you blindly increase your target profit, it could take months or even years for the stock to reach your target. Case in point, as of this writing, Charles Schwab Corporation (SCHW) is trading around $82. Now, you can have a $10 stop loss and a $100 target profit. But here's the thing. Over the last 10 years, SCHW has increased $70 in price. How many years do you think it'll take for the price to increase $100?

Clearly, you can't just blindly reduce your stop loss or increase your target profit if you want to achieve a favorable risk to reward on the trade. So what now?

Proper stop loss and reasonable target

The key here is to choose a proper stop loss so you don't get stopped out by the slightest noise in the market and to determine a reasonable target that the stock could reach within the next few days or weeks (assuming you're trading on the daily timeframe). Here's what I mean...

Figure 11.1 – Stop loss 1 ATR below support

1. Amazon.com (AMZN) is in an uptrend.
2. The stock then makes a pullback towards the swing low around $146.
3. Next, the price forms a bullish reversal pattern (bullish engulfing pattern) and closes at $149.

Now, how do you assess the potential risk to reward on the trade? First, you need to know your stop loss level. If you recall, your stop loss can go 1 ATR below the low of the bullish reversal pattern. The low of the bullish reversal pattern is $141, and the current ATR value is $5.64. So, you'll set your stop loss at $135.36 (calculation: $141.00 - $5.64 = $135.36).

Second, you need to calculate the distance of your stop loss. Let's assume the market opens the next day at $5.99 and you enter at that price. Recall that the distance of your stop loss is calculated as entry price minus stop loss level. This means the distance of your stop loss is $0.91 (calculation $5.99 - $5.08 = $0.91).

Third, you want to calculate the distance of your target profit. This is calculated as target profit level minus entry price. So let's say you want to exit your trade at $7.10 (before opposing pressure steps in at the recent swing high). This means the distance of your target profit is $1.11 (calculation: $7.10 - $5.99 = $1.11).

Finally, to assess your risk-to-reward ratio, just divide the distance of your target profit by the distance of your stop loss. So you get $1.11 / $0.93 = 1.19.

In other words, this trade offers a potential risk to reward of 1:1.19. Does this make sense? Now you might be thinking…

"SO WHAT'S THE MINIMUM RISK-TO-REWARD RATIO I SHOULD AIM FOR?"

There's no minimum risk-to-reward ratio. As you know, your risk-to-reward ratio is only one side of the equation. The other element is your winning rate. Thus you can have a risk-to-reward ratio of 1:0.5, but if your winning rate is high enough, you can still be a profitable trader.

Generally, for swing traders, you have a higher winning rate so your risk-to-reward ratio can be anywhere from 1:1 up to 1:1.5.

For trend followers, you will have a lower winning rate so your risk-to-reward ratio is anywhere from 1:2 up to 1:4.

Now, you should take these guidelines with a pinch of salt because every trader is different, and your numbers may or may not be within the same range. If in doubt, refer to the expectancy formula, so you'll know whether or not your trading strategy will make money in the long run.

At this point, you've learned what the risk-to-reward ratio is and how it works. Next, we'll analyze a few trading examples so you can get a better idea of how the theory works in the real world of trading.

SUMMARY

- Risk-to-reward ratio is used to measure your risk relative to your return (also known as the R multiple).

- Identifying favorable risk-to-reward trading setups involves setting a proper stop loss away from the noise of the market, along with a reasonable target profit.

- On its own, the risk-to-reward ratio is meaningless. You need to look at both your risk-to-reward ratio and your winning rate to know if you'll make money in the long run.

STOCK TRADING STRATEGIES
that work

When I was in university, I had a lecturer who taught economics. In the first lesson, she spent two hours asking us, "What is economics?" She went through stuff like allocation of resources, economies of scale, productivity, and so on. Imagine a lecturer spending two hours going back and forth, trying to make us understand what economics was.

In the next lesson, she did the same thing! After that, I started skipping her class. Why? Because I didn't see how what she was teaching us could be applied to the exams. This taught me the importance of understanding not only the theory but also how to apply it.

Now, this applies to learning how to trade. You can understand all the fancy concepts, techniques, or whatever. But if you can't apply them in the real world of trading, then what's the point?

That's why, right now, I want to help you piece together the types of puzzles that can come up, so you can apply them to the real world of trading. So let me introduce you to the TAEE formula...

THE TAEE FORMULA: A PULLBACK TRADING STRATEGY THAT WORKS

T = Trend: As you know, it's easier to make money buying stocks when they're in an uptrend. That's because they're likely to continue moving higher over the next few weeks or months. So, the first thing you want to do is find stocks that are in an uptrend.

A = Area of Value: Next, you want to identify the area of value so you know *where* to enter a trade. This can include determining things like support and resistance, trendlines, moving average, and so on. For example, if you're looking for buying opportunities, you'll want to ask yourself, "Where might potential buying pressure step in?"

E = Entry Trigger: Then, you'll want to have an entry trigger, so you'll know *when* to enter a trade. If you're looking for buying opportunities, you can look for candlestick patterns like the hammer, the bullish engulfing pattern, and so on.

E = Exits: Finally, you establish exits so you know *when* to exit a trade. There are two parts to this: 1) You can exit when the price moves against you (otherwise known as a stop loss); 2) You can exit when the price moves in your favor (you can do this using target profit or trailing stop loss).

All good? Then let's have a look at a few examples now…

Example 1: ProSahres UltraPro QQQ (TQQQ)

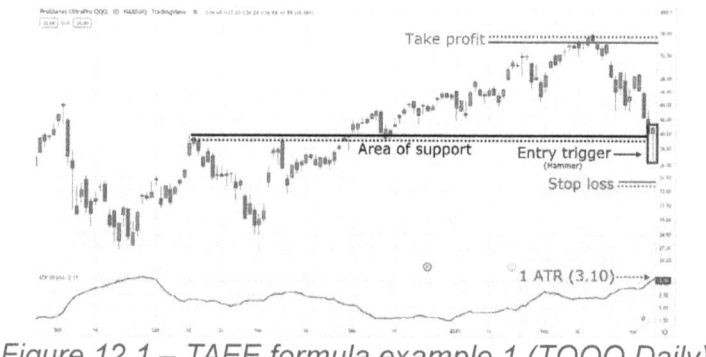

Figure 12.1 – TAEE formula example 1 (TQQQ Daily)

TQQQ was in an uptrend as the price formed a series of higher highs and lows (trend). Then, it made a pullback towards support at around $40 (area of value). Next, a hammer appeared as the price traded below the low of support only to reverse higher (entry trigger). In this scenario, you can enter at the opening of the next candle and have your stop loss 1 ATR below the low of the candle (exit if you are wrong). If you want to capture a swing, you can look to make a profit of around $55.80, which is before the nearest swing high (exit if you are right).

Now, what's the potential risk-to-reward ratio on this trade? Let's find out...

Entry price

Let's assume the market opens at the same price it closed at yesterday. So, our entry price will be $41.88.

Distance of your stop loss

Note: The low of the candle is $37.52, and the current ATR value is $3.10.

You want to set your stop loss one ATR below the low of the candle. In this case, it'll be $34.42 (calculation: $37.52 - $3.10 = $34.42).

So, the distance of your stop loss from entry is $3.10 (calculation: $37.52 - $34.42 = $3.10).

Distance of your target profit

Note: The nearest swing high is $19.10.

You want to exit your trade before opposing pressure steps in. In this case, it's before the nearest swing high, so let's set it at $18.50.

So the distance of your target profit from entry is $3.43 (calculation: $18.50 - $15.07 = $3.43).

Potential risk to reward

Now, to assess your potential risk to reward on the trade, just divide the distance of your target profit by the distance of your stop loss.

In this case, it's $1.99 (calculation $3.43 / $1.72 = $1.99). This means you're risking $1 to potentially make $1.99 on this trade. Next example...

Example 2: Marvell Technology (MRVL)

Figure 12.2 – TAEE formula example 2 (MRVL Daily)

MRVL is in an uptrend because the price is moving through a series of higher highs and lows (trend). Then it makes a pullback towards the 50-day moving average and support (also known as a stacked area of value because multiple areas of value overlap one another). Next, the price forms a bullish hammer, which signals that the buyers are in control (entry trigger). You can look to enter on the next day's open and have your stop loss 1 ATR below the low of the candle (exit if you are wrong). You can look to take profit before the nearest swing high, around $91 (exit if you are right).

Now, let's assume that...

- You have a $10,000 account.
- You want to risk $200 on this trade.
- The distance of your stop loss is $10.

So, how many shares of MRVL can you buy?

Recall the formula... *Position size = Amount to risk in $ / Distance of your stop loss in $*

Position size = $200 / $10

Position size = 20 shares of MRVL

This means you can buy 20 shares of MRVL, and if the stock price drops $10, you'll lose $200 on the trade.

Now, in this example, I've made the numbers easy to calculate. But in reality, you'll encounter decimals when calculating your position size. So, use a position sizing calculator to make your life easier. I've included one in the bonus resources that come with this book, which you'll find here: bonus.stocktradingbook.com

Example 3: Houghton Mifflin Harcourt Company (TWTR)

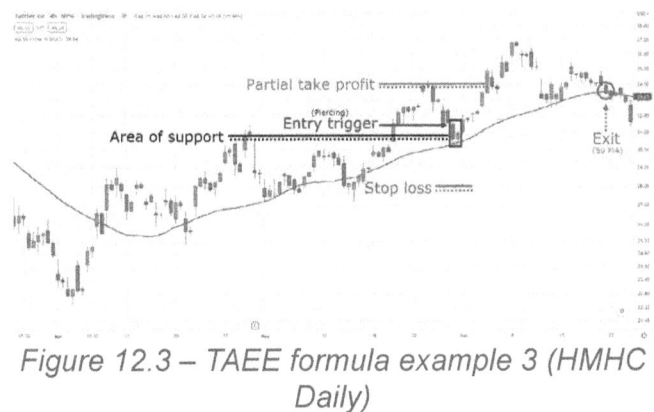

Figure 12.3 – TAEE formula example 3 (HMHC Daily)

As you can see, this looks similar to the earlier setups. And that's what trading is all about: trading the same setup consistently over and over again. So, let's go faster this time around…

TWTR is in an uptrend, and the price made a pullback towards the 50-day moving average and support, at around

$31. Then, it formed a bullish reversal pattern (also known as a piercing pattern), which is a valid entry trigger to go long. You can enter at the next day's open. If you want to capture a swing, you can exit your trade before the nearest swing high, around $34. But wait, what if you want to ride this trend higher? Then you must use a trailing stop loss. For example, you can trail your stop loss using the 50-day moving average. This means you'll exit your trade only if the price closes below the 50-day moving average; if not, you'll hold on to the trade and ride the trend higher until the price closes below the 50-day moving average.

Next, let me introduce to you another formula…

TBEE FORMULA: A BREAKOUT TRADING STRATEGY THAT WORKS

Now, this is similar to the TAEE formula but with one difference. Instead of area of value, you're looking for a buildup to form. This means you're looking for a tight consolidation to form before you trade a breakout. Here are a few examples...

Example 4: Tempur Sealy International (TPX)

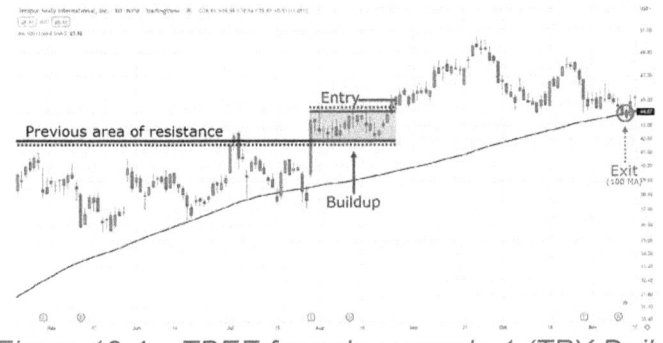

Figure 12.4 – TBEE formula example 1 (TPX Daily)

TPX recently broke above resistance at $42.50, which means the stock is in an uptrend. Then it forms a bull flag pattern (which is also a buildup), which signals buyers are stepping in to support the higher prices. Next, the price closes above the high of the bull flag, which is a valid entry trigger to go long. You can enter at the next day's open and set your stop loss 1 ATR below the low of the bull flag. Otherwise, you can use a trailing stop loss like moving average, % drop in price, or chandelier stop.

In this case, I've used a 100-day moving average. So if you were to use this setup, you'd exit your trade when the price closed below the 100-day moving average.

If you want to learn about different ways to trail your stop loss, watch the bonus training that comes with this book. You can find it here: bonus.stocktradingbook.com

Example 5: Live Nation Entertainment (LYV)

Figure 12.5 – TBEE formula example 2 (LYV Daily)

LYV recently broke above resistance at $94, meaning the stock was in an uptrend. Then it formed a bull flag pattern, signaling buyers were stepping in to support the higher prices. Next, the price closed above the high of the bull flag, which is a valid entry trigger to go long. By rights, you're supposed to enter at the next day's open, but let's say you were slow to this trade, and by the time you wanted to enter, the stock had rallied another $2 above your entry price. So, what now? Well, there are three things you can do.

1. You can skip the trade and look for other trading opportunities.

2. You can enter the trade at the current price. The good thing is you won't miss this trade. But it comes at the expense of a larger stop loss since you're buying at a higher price (compared to the original entry point).

3. You can place a buy limit order at your original entry price. If your order gets filled, it'll work out as if you hadn't missed the trade at all. However, the stock might not retrace to your buy limit order, and you'll miss the trade.

Now, there's no right or wrong answer here. This example is meant to get you thinking about options that you might not have considered.

Example 6: First Bancorp (FBP)

Figure 12.6 – TBEE formula example 3 (FBP Daily)

FBP recently broke above resistance and the stock is in an uptrend. Then it formed a bull flag pattern, where you could go long if the price broke above it.

Now, if you were to wait for a close above the high of the flag pattern, the price might close much higher than the breakout point, and you'd be buying at a higher price. So, what can you do about this? Well, you can place a buy stop order above the high of the flag pattern. This means if the stock trades one tick above the high of the flag pattern, you'll immediately enter the trade.

The advantage is that you'll enter at the breakout point, and this will be the best entry price if the stock takes off like a rocket. The downside is, it could be a false breakout, and you'll have entered the trade prematurely.

As for exits, I've used a 20% trailing stop loss in this example. For example, if you place a buy stop order at $14, then your trailing stop loss will be at $11.20 (calculation: $14 × 0.8 = $11.20). This means if the price closes below $11.20, you'll exit the trade. And if the price continues higher, you'll adjust your trailing stop loss accordingly.

Here's a quick example. Let's say the stock price reaches a high of $20. Then your new trailing stop loss will be $16, and you'll exit the trade if the price closes below it. Does this make sense?

Now you might be wondering, "Why didn't you show the outcome of these trades?" I didn't do this because the results of these examples are random. Heck, I could show you seven winners and three losers, but would it mean this strategy had a 70% winning rate? Of course not. The purpose of these examples is to teach you the thought process behind them, so you can adjust these strategies to your needs, and then go "hunt" on your own. Cool? Moving on…

STOCK SCANNER: HOW DO YOU QUICKLY SCAN FOR TRADING

OPPORTUNITIES?

There are thousands of stocks out there, and it doesn't make sense to sift through chart by chart to look for stocks that are in an uptrend. So is there a faster way to do things? Yes! You can use a stock scanner to make your life easier. There are many stock scanners out there, and I won't list them here because by the time this book is published, some of these scanners might no longer be around. Regardless what scanner you end up using, here are the settings I use to scan for trading opportunities…

- The stock price achieved a new 52-week high.
- The stock price has increased at least 100% over the last 12 months (this can be adjusted higher/lower if no stocks are showing up).
- The market capitalization is at

least $1 billion.
- The average volume is at least one million.

Now, I run the scanner daily to find stocks that have achieved a new 52-week high. Chances are, they are in an uptrend, and I can decide if they fit into any category (whether it's a strong trend, a healthy trend, or a weak trend). If they fit, I add them to my watchlist.

If you do this for a month, you'll build your own watchlist of stocks to trade. I've added a training video that shows you how I scan for stock trading opportunities every day. You can get it in the bonus resources that come with this book. Here's the link: bonus.stocktradingbook.com.

At this point, you've learned the TAEE and TBEE formulas, so you understand how to trade a pullback or a breakout. I've also shared several trading examples with you, so you know when to enter and exit your trades. In the next chapter, I'll share a few secrets that can help you further increase your winning rate.

SUMMARY

- The TAEE formula is used to trade pullbacks. The letters in the acronym stand for trend, area of value, entry trigger, and exit.

- The TBEE formula is used to trade a breakout. The letters in the acronym stand for trend, buildup, entry trigger, and exit.

TRADE SWEETENERS

Imagine you're chasing after a girl called Michelle. You don't have many similar interests, and you struggle to find common topics to talk about. Let me ask you, what are the odds of you getting together with Michelle? Your chances are probably slim. Agree?

Next, let's say you're chasing another girl called Sarah. You and Sarah have common interests and you can talk about technology, fashion, cars, and a whole range of other topics. Now, what are the odds of you getting together with Sarah? Pretty good, if you ask me (as long as you're not friend-zoned).

As you can see, if you and the person you're chasing after have similar interests, you have better odds of winning them over—and the same goes for trading. If you have multiple factors in your favor, you increase the odds of the trade working out. So here are some trade sweeteners (a term that refers to a price pattern or technique) to help you do just that...

POWER AND DIVERGENCE (PAD)

This technique is used to identify strength in a stock when there's short-term weakness in the stock market. Here's what to look for...

- The S&P 500 had a lower close.
- The stock had a higher close and forms a bullish reversal candlestick pattern (like a hammer or a bullish engulfing pattern).

Here's an example...

Example 1-1: S&P 500 closed lower for the day

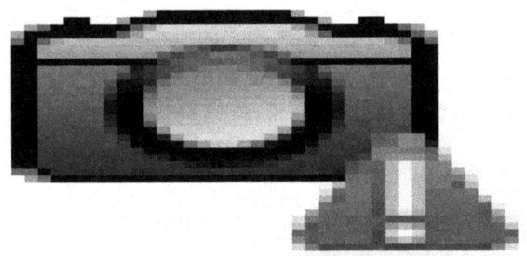

Figure 13.1 – S&P 500 closed lower for the day

The S&P 500 is in an uptrend and closes lower for the day. When this happens, you shouldn't be surprised to find that most stocks have closed lower as well.

Example 1-2: Advanced Micro Devices Inc. (AMD) made a pullback and closed higher for the day

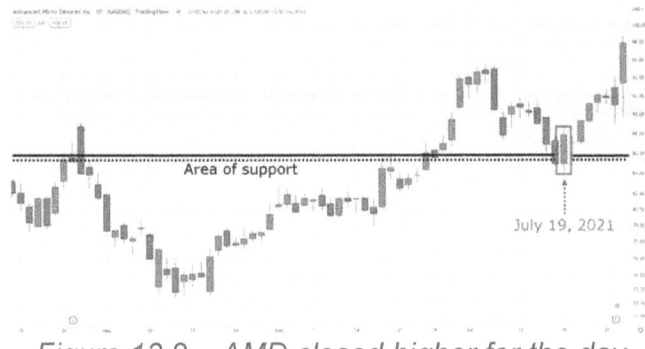

Figure 13.2 – AMD closed higher for the day

On the same day, AMD was in an uptrend, and the price made a pullback towards support (at around $86). Even though the stock market index closed lower for the day, AMD formed a bullish reversal candlestick pattern and closed higher for the day (the opposite of the stock market index). This is an example of power and divergence (PAD). It signals that buying pressure is pushing the stock higher and could continue to do so over the next few days.

(I won't go into detail about entry, stop loss, and exits, as we covered these earlier.)

This is a powerful concept, so let me walk you through a few more examples…

Example 2-1: S&P 500 closed lower for the day

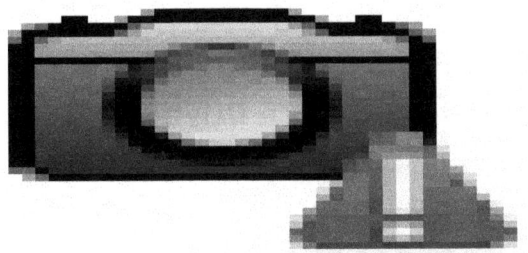

Figure 13.3 – S&P 500 closed lower for the day

The S&P 500 is in an uptrend and closed lower for the day.

Example 2-2: Cloudflare (NET) made a pullback and closed higher for the day

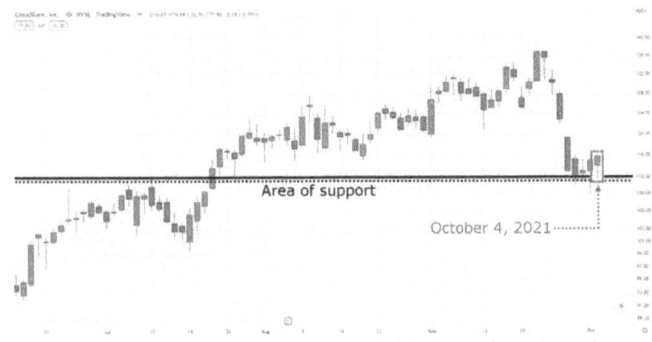

Figure 13.4 – NET closed higher for the day

On the same day, NET was in an uptrend, and the stock made a pullback towards support (at around $110). On this day, most stocks were expected to close lower for the day, but not NET. It formed a bullish hammer and closed higher. This meant buying pressure was stepping in, even when the overall market was down for the day. Now, the PAD concept doesn't apply only to pullback trading because it can also work for breakout trades. Let me give you an example...

Example 3-1: S&P 500 closed lower for the day

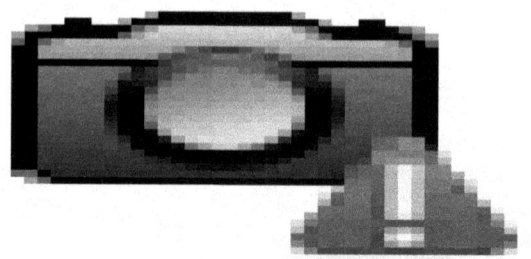

Figure 13.5 – S&P 500 closed lower for the day

The S&P 500 was in an uptrend and closed lower for the day.

Example 3-2: Avis Budget Group (CAR) broke out of resistance

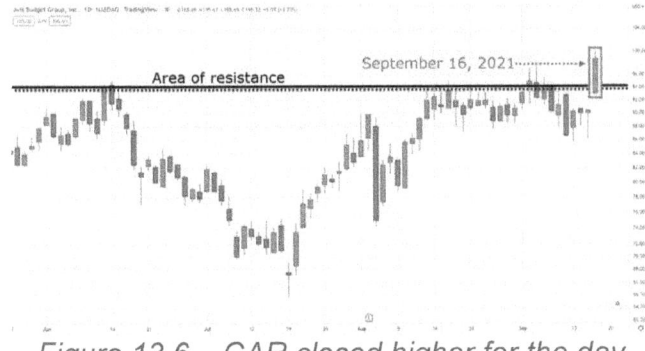

Figure 13.6 – CAR closed higher for the day

On the same day, CAR was in an uptrend and formed a buildup at resistance (at around $96). Unlike the stock market index, it broke out of resistance and closed higher for the day. This is a sign of strength, and the stock price could continue higher over the next few days. Let's have a look at one last example...

Example 4-1: S&P 500 closed lower for the day

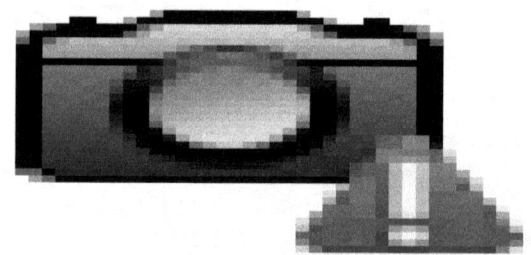

Figure 13.7 – S&P 500 closed lower for the day

The S&P 500 was in an uptrend and closed lower for the day. I sound like a broken recording, but you get the idea now.

Example 4-2: Crocs (CROX) broke out of resistance

Figure 13.8 – CROX closed higher for the day

On the same day, CROX was in an uptrend and broke out of the swing high (at around $148)—closing higher for the day. This is a sign of strength, and the stock price could continue higher over the next few days.

Moving on, let's learn about another trade sweetener…

PICK THE STRONGER STOCK

There are times when you have two similar trading setups, and you can't decide which one to choose. So what now? One way to decide is to pick the stronger of the two stocks. Why? As you've learned, strong-performing stocks are likely to continue moving higher over the next few weeks or months. Thus, you want to select the strongest-performing stocks when you're spoiled for choice. One way to do this is using the rate of change (ROC) indicator.

The ROC indicator measures the percentage change in price. So if you use a 100-day ROC, you're using an indicator that measures the stock's price change over the past 100 days. Here's an example...

- Apple stock is currently trading at $180.
- A hundred days ago, Apple stock was trading at $150.

So what's the rate of change over the last 100 days?

Well, the ROC value is 20 because Apple gained 20% over the last 100 days (calculation: [180 - 150] / 150 = 0.2).

And here's how to do it on your charting platform...

1. Calculate the 100-day rate-of-change (ROC) indicator for both stocks.
2. Pick the stock with the higher ROC value.

Here's an example...

Example 5-1: Canadian Natural Resources (CNQ), ROC value of 43.65

Figure 13.9 – Rate of change (ROC) value of 43.65

CNQ had a breakout, and its 100-day ROC value is 43.65. At the same time, you notice another breakout trading setup on Nucor Corporation (NUE)...

Example 5-2: Nucor Corporation (NUE) Roc value of 34.38

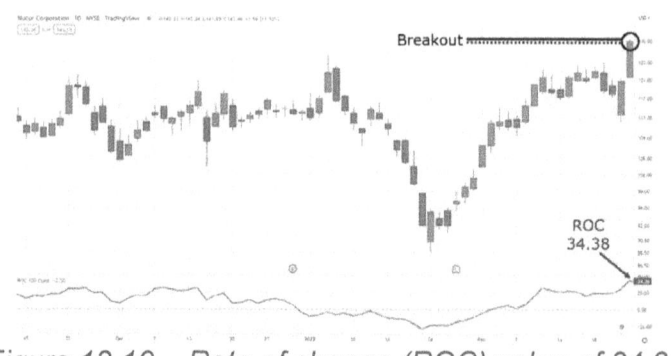

Figure 13.10 – Rate of change (ROC) value of 34.38

As you can see, NUE has an ROC value of 34.38. Let's say you can only pick one of these two stocks to trade. Which should you go for? The answer is CNQ because it has a higher ROC value. Make sense?

Now you might be wondering, "Why use the 100-day rate of change?" Well, that's because it's an easy number to remember. On a more serious note, according to research and backtesting, stocks that have performed well over the last 3 to 12 months are likely to continue higher. So a 100-day rate of change covers that lookback period (a 100-day ROC covers a lookback period of 5 months because there are about 20 trading days in a month).

Of course, you can also use a 200-day ROC, a 250-day ROC, and so on. As long as the lookback period covers the last 3 to 12 months, it's fine. Moving on...

POWER BREAKOUT

Here's the deal: when the stock market index breaks out higher, most stocks will follow suit. However, there are times when the stocks break out before the stock market index does. So, what's the deal? Well, these are leaders in the stock market, and they are likely to go higher and further. The key is to look for stocks that break out and start moving higher ahead of the stock market index. Here's an example...

Example 6-1: S&P 500 is below the highest high (25 February 2022)

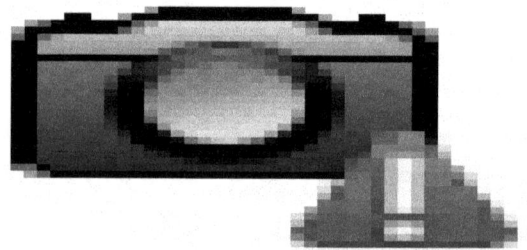

Figure 13.11 – S&P 500 very much below the highest high

The S&P 500 closed bullishly higher. However, it's below the highest high (at around $4800).

Example 6-2: Canadian Natural Resources (CNQ) broke out higher

Figure 13.12 – CNQ broke out higher

On the same day, CNQ was in an uptrend and broke out higher after it formed an ascending triangle pattern (a variation of a buildup). This stock is a market leader, as it didn't break out at the same time as the stock market—it broke out before the stock market did.

Now imagine, the overall market becomes bullish and moves higher. A stock market leader (like CNQ) is likely to go even higher. And if the overall market is in a downturn, the stock market leader isn't likely to fall that far. That's the beauty of identifying a power breakout.

Example 7-1: S&P 500 is below the highest high and closed lower for the day

Figure 13.13 – S&P 500 is below the highest high

The S&P 500 is below the highest high (at around $4800) and closed lower for the day.

Example 7-2: Alcoa (AA) broke out higher

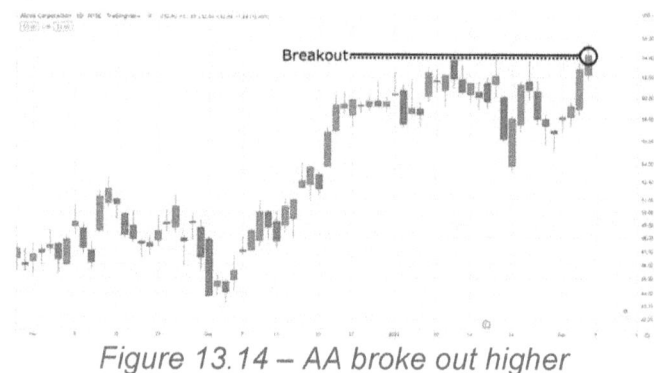

Figure 13.14 – AA broke out higher

On the same day, Alcoa (AA) broke out higher—another example of a power breakout. Also, there's a power and divergence sweetener (PAD) since Alcoa closed higher for the day, while S&P 500 closed lower. This makes the trade even sweeter. Does this make sense?

At this point, you've learned about powerful trade sweeteners that can help you identify high-probability trading setups. In the next chapter, you'll learn how to develop a trading plan so you can continuously improve your trading results.

SUMMARY

- Power and divergence (PAD) occurs when the stock market index closes lower but the individual stock closes higher.

- If there are two similar trading setups, go with the stronger stock. One way to decide is to pick the stock that has the higher rate of change (ROC) over the last 100 days.

- Power breakout occurs when a stock has broken out higher, but the stock market index hasn't.

HOW TO DEVELOP A TRADING PLAN to improve your trading results

When I got home one day, I saw my son, Rae, running through the house naked. His "bird" was flapping up and down, and this wasn't appropriate. So I asked Rae, "Why are you running around the house naked? Do you want me to say hello to your bird?"

Then Rae marched up to me, looked me in the eye, and placed his hands on his "bird." He shook it vigorously, and said hello to me while shaking it! I was dumbfounded and didn't know how to react. Before I could say anything, Rae ran off again with the "flapping bird."

Now here's the thing. Often the markets will leave you dumbfounded by doing a whole lot of whatever you least expect. And when you're caught off guard by the markets, you'll let your emotions take control, and that usually leads to a worse outcome. That's why you must have a trading plan to cover all contingencies no matter what the market does to you.

You might be wondering, "What's a trading plan?" Well, it's a set of rules to guide your trading so you know exactly what to do in any market condition.

Here are the benefits of having a trading plan:

- You'll face fewer emotional roller coasters and you'll be better able to manage your fears.
- You'll respond with less subjectivity, which means you'll get more consistent results.
- You'll be able to handle anything the market throws at you, which will make you a more confident

trader.

Now that you understand the importance of a trading plan, I'll tell you how to develop one for yourself.

HOW TO DEVELOP A TRADING PLAN

Here are four things you must have in every trading plan:

1. Timeframe

For new traders, I recommend trading the daily timeframe because you'll have ample time to plan your decisions each day.

This is perfect for people who are working full-time, studying, or running a business.

Unlike the Forex market, where you get fewer trading opportunities on the daily timeframe because there are only a limited number of currencies to trade, the stock market is different. There are thousands of stocks out there, and you can find plenty of trading opportunities.

Of course, as you mature as a trader, you can trade across different timeframes. But for starters, stick to one timeframe so you don't confuse yourself. Next…

2. Market capitalization

Since there are thousands of stocks out there, how do you know which types of stocks to trade? One way is to filter stocks according to their market capitalization.

For starters, you can look at stocks with a market capitalization of at least $10 billion. These stocks are more liquid, which means you can easily enter and exit your trades—with minimal slippage.

3. Risk

As you know, trading is about probabilities, not certainties. Thus, every trade you make has a probability of being a loser. The last thing you want is to have one losing trade wipe out your account. The solution? You risk a small fraction of your capital on each trade.

As a general rule, you can strive not to risk more than 1% of your account on each trade. This means, if your account size is $100,000, you'll lose no more than $1,000 per trade (calculation: 0.01 × $100,000 = $1,000).

4. Setup

The setup refers to the exact market conditions under which you'll enter and exit your trade. In this case, you can use an "if-then" template to define your trading setup. Here's an example…

If the stock is in an uptrend, then I'll wait for it to move towards an area of value (like support).

If the stock moves towards an area of value, then I'll look for an entry trigger to go long (like a hammer).

If I see a valid entry trigger, then I'll enter on the next candle open and set my stop loss 1 ATR below the swing low.

If the price moves in my favor, I'll exit my trade before the nearest swing high.

Finally, let me show you an example of what a trading plan looks like…

Trading plan example

Timeframe: Daily

Market capitalization: $10 billion and above

Risk: I won't risk more than 1% of my trading account.

My trading setup is as follows…

If the stock is in an uptrend, then I'll wait for it to move towards an area of value (like support).

If the stock moves towards an area of value, then I'll look for an entry trigger to go long (like a hammer).

If I see a valid entry trigger, then I'll enter on the next candle open and set my stop loss 1 ATR below the swing low.

If the price moves in my favor, I'll exit my trade before the nearest swing high.

Once you've developed your trading plan, then it's time to move on to the next step…

EXECUTE THE TRADES ACCORDING TO YOUR TRADING PLAN

When you execute your trades, it's important to follow your trading plan. That's because a consistent set of actions leads to consistent results. And your trading plan is what keeps your actions consistent—don't forget that.

In addition, you must continue to execute your trades even if you encounter a series of losing trades. Why? In the short run, your trading results are random (in the same way tossing a coin can come up heads five times in a row, even though the odds are supposed to be 50-50). This means you need a larger sample size of trades before you can conclude whether or not your trading strategy works. Does this make sense?

As you execute your trades, one of five things can happen:

1. Small win
2. Large win
3. Small loss
4. Large loss
5. Breakeven

The key here is to eliminate large losses through proper risk management. If you can do that, you're much closer to becoming a profitable trader. Moving on…

RECORD YOUR TRADES

Let me ask you this: Do you remember what you ate for breakfast yesterday? What about last Wednesday? What did you have for breakfast? How about 30 days ago? What did you have for dinner? I'm sure you're having difficulty recalling this. Well, the same goes for trading.

You probably don't remember the details of your last 10 trades. And if you don't, how can you improve things? That's why it's important to record every trade you make. Here are the metrics that you should record...

Date – The date you entered your trade

Stock – The stock you traded

Timeframe – The timeframe you entered on

Setup – The setup (or strategy) you used

Entry price – The price you entered at

Stop loss – Your stop-loss level

Exit price – The price you exited your trade at

R multiple – This refers to how much you gained or lost relative to your risk on the trade. For example, if you risked $100 and earned $200, that's a gain of 2R (calculation: $200 / $100 = $2). Likewise, if you risked $100 and lost $100, that's a loss of 1R (calculation: -$100 / $100 = $1)

Screen capture your entry – This refers to recording the chart at the point you entered a trade.

Screen capture your exit – This refers to recording the chart at the point you exited a trade.

These are just the basic metrics you should record. You can also take things a step further and record details like the time of day you entered a trade, how you were feeling, and so on—it's entirely up to you.

Next, you're probably wondering, "What am I going to do with all this information I'm recording?" Well, recording details of your trades allows you to review them and improve your trading results. Here's how...

REVIEW YOUR TRADES

When you review your trades, ideally, you'll want to have 100 trades made with the same trading setup. Why? Because, in the short run, your trading results are random. And in the long run, you'll be able to see whether your trading strategy is working or not (after taking into account the law of large numbers). That's why you'll want to review a large sample size of trades before coming to a conclusion. However, it takes awhile to get up to 100 trades (especially if you're on the higher timeframe). So, as a bare minimum, make at least 30 trades first before doing a review. Once you've made that many, here's what to look for...

Winning rate

This refers to how often you win. For example, if you made 100 trades and won 60 of them, then your winning rate is 60% (calculation: 60 / 100 = 0.6).

There's no ideal winning rate because it depends on your trading strategy. For example, a trend follower could be using a strategy with a winning rate of 40% but still be profitable as a result of large infrequent wins, whereas a swing trader could have a 60% winning rate and profit from small consistent wins.

Anyway, if your winning rate is below the norm, here are a few things you can do:

1. Understand the big picture

Let me ask you this: If the overall market is in a recession or a downtrend, won't it be difficult to make money buying stocks? Can you see how this works?

This means you only want to look for trading opportunities when the overall market is in an uptrend (or at most, in a range). Avoid buying stocks when the overall market is in a downtrend. But how?

One way is to use the 200-day moving average as a trend filter. This means if the stock market index (like the S&P 500) is above the 200-day moving average, you look for buying opportunities in stocks. If it's below the 200-day moving average, remain in cash.

This way, you trade when the overall market is in an uptrend and avoid getting slaughtered in a downtrend or a recession.

2. Buy stocks that are trending higher

Avoid taking trades when the stock is choppy or directionless. Instead, identify stocks that are in an uptrend and trade in the direction of the uptrend.

3. Trade from an area of value

Don't chase the market. Instead, let the market come to you. This puts the odds in your favor and offers you a more favorable risk to reward.

4. Look for trade sweeteners

Earlier, you learned about trade sweeteners, like power and divergence and power breakout, which help increase your winning rate. So go hunt for them in your trading setups. Yes, you might have fewer trading opportunities as these are sweeteners that don't come around that often. But hey, your goal as a trader isn't to trade as much as possible, it's to trade only when the odds are in your favor. Right?

5. Have a reasonable stop loss

If your stop loss is too tight, you'll likely get stopped out before the market even has a chance to move in your favor. So, give your trade room to breathe and set a proper stop loss. The principle is to have your stop loss at a level that, if reached, will invalidate your trading setup. And if your stop loss is so large that it doesn't justify the risk to reward on the trade, then give the trade a miss.

6. Have a reasonable target profit

If your target profit is too high, the trade is unlikely to reach it. So, set a reasonable target profit that the price has a likelihood of reaching. This is usually before price structure like swing high and low, support and resistance, etc.

Patterns that lead to winners

This is a technique I learned from a guy called Tom Dante (he can be found on Twitter with the handle @Trader_Dante). The idea is simple.

Once you've screenshotted a list of trading setups, you can then review them and identify patterns that lead to your winners. You want to ask yourself, "Is there some pattern that my winners have in common?" If you see something, record it. Then, update your trading plan accordingly and take into account this pattern when you trade in the future.

Patterns that lead to losers

Likewise, you want to identify patterns that lead to your losers. Imagine there's a certain pattern that likely results in a losing trade—and you can avoid it. How much better would your results be? So, start reviewing your trades and hunt those patterns down.

At this point, you've learned how to develop a trading plan, record your trades, and review them so you can improve your trading results. Next, you'll learn how to choose a good stockbroker you can trust your money with.

SUMMARY

- A trading plan is a fixed set of rules that will guide your trading so you can become a consistent trader.

- Your trading plan should state the timeframe, market capitalization of stocks you are trading, risk per trade, and details of your trading setup.

- Your trading journal should have metrics like the date, stock, timeframe, setup, entry price, stop-loss level, exit price, and R multiple—plus screenshots of your setup (before and after the trade).

- Review your trades so you can find ways to improve. You can identify patterns that lead to your winners and focus on these aspects of your trading setup.

Likewise, you can identify patterns that lead to your losers and avoid these aspects of your trading setup.

HOW TO CHOOSE A GOOD
stockbroker

My first stockbroker was a local broker called DBS Vickers. I had an existing relationship with DBS bank, and it just seemed natural to open an account with their stockbroking arm (after all, I was already familiar with them).

DBS Vickers wasn't the best or the worst broker, but it worked well enough to get me started. So does this mean you should do something similar? No, because there's a better way to do it, and it starts with looking for these things in a stockbroker…

IS THE BROKER REGULATED IN THE CORRECT COUNTRIES?

When a stockbroker is regulated, it means there's a watchdog overseeing them to ensure they don't do anything funny (like stealing your money). However, not all regulators are the same.

The good ones are strict and will enforce rules (like having sufficient capital, audit checks, etc.) to protect their citizens. The bad ones? They do nothing and traders get screwed.

As a general rule, go with brokers who are regulated in Singapore, the US, the UK, or Australia.

GOOD SUPPORT AND SERVICE

The stock brokerage industry is hugely competitive, and the better brokers will offer you good service and support because they have the resources to do so.

So how do you define good service and support? If you ask me, your broker should have live chat support 24/5, from Monday to Friday.

This way, even if you can't access your trading platform, you can still manage your positions quickly.

EASY WITHDRAWAL

These days, money can be quickly moved anywhere. So if you want to withdraw your funds, it shouldn't take more than five business days.

My suggestion is that you fund your account with a small sum of money—and then withdraw it. If you get your money back fast, you can consider adding more funds.

If you don't get your money back, then hey, you just saved yourself a ton of money.

MARKETS OFFERED

All stockbrokers will allow you to trade stocks. Duh. But if you want to trade other instruments like options, futures, exchange-traded funds (ETFs), and so on, you must check whether or not your broker offers these (there's no guarantee it will).

TRANSACTION COSTS

There are two types of stockbrokers. Those who charge you a commission on every trade and those with zero commission. So does this mean you should go with commission-free brokers since you can trade for free? Well, it depends.

The way zero-commission stockbrokers earn their money is primarily by selling your order flow to high-frequency trading (HFT) firms. I won't go into details here, but the implication is, you might not get the best possible prices with zero-commission stockbrokers. This may or may not matter to you depending what type of trader you are. So, as a general rule...

If you're a new trader, your frequency of trades is low, and your holding duration is months or even years, then yes, commission-free stockbrokers are fine to use because they won't affect your trading too much.

But if you're an advanced trader, you trade frequently, and your holding duration is usually days, then go with a stockbroker that doesn't sell your order flow because you'll notice your fills on your trade are much better compared to a zero-commission stockbroker.

Now, I get it. There's a lot to consider when you're choosing a stockbroker. So, if you want my recommendation, you can find it at bonus.stocktradingbook.com

At this point, you've learned how to choose a good stockbroker. Next, you'll discover some of the most common stock trading mistakes and how to avoid them.

SUMMARY

- When you decide it's time to find a stockbroker, make sure the broker you choose
    1. is regulated in the correct countries
    2. offers good service and support
    3. allows you to withdraw your money easily
    4. offers the instruments you want
    5. has a transaction cost structure that meets your needs

SEVEN COMMON STOCK TRADING MISTAKES to avoid

It was April 2020 and crude oil was trading at a multi-year low (around $30). There were two reasons for this: COVID-19 had struck and travel was restricted. This meant airplanes couldn't fly, so oil demand was low. Next, oil producers were still pumping oil out, and that led to an oversupply of oil. So when demand is low and supply is high, what happens? Prices drop—and that's what happened to the price of oil.

Now this was my thought process back then: "We will survive COVID-19. And when things get better, travel restrictions will be lifted and airplanes will resume flying. Oil demand will eventually return in three to five years." So what did I do? I went long on crude oil. I bought $100,000 worth of West Texas Intermediate (WTI) crude oil at around $21. I planned to hold it for the next three to five years because I thought oil had the potential to double or triple in price. But Mr. Market had other plans for me…

On April 20, 2020, there was huge selling pressure on oil. It got so bad that the price of crude oil went negative—to the tune of negative $37. Yes, you read me right. Crude oil was trading at negative $37, which meant that a seller would have to pay a buyer $37 to buy crude oil. Crazy. I was caught off guard and my $100,000 position on crude oil went to zero. That episode taught me that I should have diversified my oil position into oil ETFs, Brent Crude Oil, and so on.

But here's the thing. Mistakes can't be entirely avoided because they're part of the learning process, no matter what you do. But I hope to highlight a few common stock trading mistakes that you can avoid so you don't end up paying the market hefty "tuition fees." Ready? Let's dive in...

MISTAKE 1: BUYING WEAK STOCKS

It's been statistically proven that strong stocks are likely to outperform weak stocks. This means stocks that break out to all-time highs are more likely to continue moving higher than stocks that break down to all-time lows.

Put another way, you want to buy stocks in an uptrend because they're likely to continue moving higher, and you want to avoid stocks that are in a downtrend. Yes, I know, it's psychologically easier to buy cheap stocks because it seems like you're getting "value" for your money. However, remember that what's cheap can become cheaper. So do you want to buy a cheap stock or a stock with a better chance of moving higher? Use data to guide your decisions, not your emotions.

MISTAKE 2: FORCING A TRADE

There are thousands of stocks you can potentially trade. But here's the thing. There are times when there's nothing to do in the market—especially during a recession or a financial crisis. Why? Because the stock market is likely to be in a downtrend along with most of the stocks.

Now there might be a few defensive stocks that are still moving higher, and if there's a valid trading setup, feel free to trade it. But if there's nothing to buy, remain on the sidelines because you'd rather be in cash than watching your account bleed day after day. Jesse Livermore once said, "There is a time to go long. There is a time to go short. And there is a time to go fishing."

MISTAKE 3: THINKING THE STOCK IS TOO HIGH TO BUY

Take a look at the chart below…

Figure 16.1 – The stock price seems high

Antero Resources is trading near the 52-week high around $16. At this point, many traders would be thinking to themselves, "The stock price is too high, it'll likely reverse and won't go any higher." But guess what?

Antero resources went up another 200% in nine months (and it's trading around $48 at the time of writing). Here's what I mean…

Figure 16.2 – A stock price that looks high can become higher

So the lesson is this. What's high can go higher—a stock is never too high to buy.

MISTAKE 4: TRADING WITHOUT A PLAN

The reason you have a trading plan is because you need a compass to guide your trading decisions. Without one, your emotions will control your trading. And as you know by now, letting your emotions dictate your actions will have disastrous effects on your trading results. This explains why you revenge trade, chase the market, and do things that leave you wondering, "Why did I do that?"

By now, I hope you understand how important a trading plan is because without one, trading is like going into a jungle without a map and compass. Do you think you'll be able to find your way out? Unlikely—and it's the same for trading.

MISTAKE 5: STRATEGY HOPPING

The first strategy I learned was a Bollinger Bands trading strategy. I was taught to buy near the low of the Bollinger Band and sell near the high. I had some success at the start, but the losses slowly crept in, and I concluded the strategy didn't work. So I moved on to the next trading strategy…

Then I came across harmonic patterns, and I learned how to draw complex chart patterns that I could use to pinpoint reversals in the market. Again, after a series of losses, I gave up and moved on to the next trading strategy I could get my hands on.

This process rinse-repeated itself until I realized my folly. I was hopping from one trading strategy to the next. But before giving myself a chance to find out whether or not a trading strategy worked, I'd abandon it and move on to the next "shiny object." In doing this, I wasted years going around in circles, with no end in sight.

So don't make the same mistake I did. Don't hop from one trading strategy to the next. Instead, adopt a trading strategy, test it, and find out if it works or not by journaling your trades. If it doesn't work, you can consider moving on to something else. But don't abandon a strategy after only a few losing trades because in the short run, your results are random.

MISTAKE 6: LOOKING FOR THE BEST TRADING STRATEGY

Here's the deal: there's no such thing as the best trading strategy, indicators, technique, or whatever. There are two reasons for this. First, the word "best" is subjective. How do you define it? The strategy that makes the most profit? The strategy with the lowest level of drawdown? The most favorable risk-to-reward ratio? If you ask 100 traders how to define the "best" trading strategy, you'll get 200 answers.

Second, market conditions change. A trading strategy that works well in one particular market condition is unlikely to work in a different market condition. For example, a trend trading strategy works well in a trending market. But, when the market starts to get choppy or goes into a range, this strategy stops working.

However, the good news is this. You don't need the best trading strategy, indicators, tools, or whatever to become a profitable trader. Instead, you need to identify market conditions that are favorable for your trading strategy and exploit them to the fullest. When market conditions change, play good defense so you can live to fight another day. And for advanced traders, you can even adopt multiple trading strategies so you can profit under different market conditions. Does this make sense?

MISTAKE 7: NO RISK MANAGEMENT

Imagine you've identified a trading setup in which all the stars are aligned (fundamentals, technical, and sentiment). You're so confident of this trade that you risk 50% of your account on it. You're thinking, "If the stock price moves in my favor, I could easily double or triple my account in one trade. Sweet!"

But then the stock goes against you, and you're down 50%. At this point, you need a gain of 100% to get back to breakeven. So you tell yourself, "I'll risk all my capital on the next trade. If the stock moves in my favor, I can quickly get back to breakeven." Unfortunately, this trade turns out to be a loser as well, and now you've blown up your account.

Here's the thing. Trading is not about taking big risks to make big returns. Instead, you should risk small, survive the ups and downs, and compound your gains over time—that's how you make it big.

At this point, you've learned seven common stock trading mistakes to avoid. Next, I'd like to share some final words with you before bringing this book to a close.

SUMMARY

- Focus on buying strong-performing stocks (those that are trending higher) and avoid the weak ones.

- There are times when there's nothing to do, especially during a bear market or a recession. Stay in cash and don't force a trade.

- A stock is never too high to buy. What's high can go higher.

- Trading without a plan can cause you to make emotional decisions—this is detrimental to your account.

- Don't hop from one trading strategy to the next. Instead, adopt a trading strategy, test it, and find out if it works or not. If it doesn't, then you can consider tweaking it or moving on to something else altogether.

- There's no such thing as the best trading strategy, indicators, settings, or whatever.
- Don't risk too much per trade because if you do, it's only a matter of time before you blow up your trading account.

Milton Keynes UK
Ingram Content Group UK Ltd.
UKHW020640220124
436466UK00019B/956